The Year of the
THISTLE
Scotland's Grand Slam 1983-84

The Year of the
THISTLE
Scotland's Grand Slam 1983-84

NORMAN MAIR

WILLOW BOOKS
Collins
8 Grafton Street, London W1
1984

To my late brother Kenneth
than whom Scotland never
had a greater supporter

Willow Books
William Collins Sons & Co. Ltd
London · Glasgow · Sydney · Auckland
Toronto · Johannesburg

Mair, Norman
   The year of the thistle: Scotland's
   Grand Slam 1983–84
   1. Rugby football – Scotland – History
   – 20th century
   I Title
   796.33'375   GV945.9.G7
ISBN 0-00-218150-9

Set in Linotron Sabon by
Rowland Phototypesetting Ltd,
Bury St Edmunds, Suffolk
Printed and bound in Great Britain
by Wm Collins Sons & Co Ltd, Glasgow

Contents

_____ Author's Preface _____

I should like to thank George Outram & Co Ltd and the _Glasgow Herald_ for permission to use material which has previously appeared under their auspices with particular reference to the chapter, A Players' Game. I am similarly indebted to John Wisden & Co Ltd for the selected extracts culled from their 1925–26 _Rugby Football Almanack_.

Then there are the six contributors: Bill Lothian, who compiled the potted biographies, and Clem Thomas, David Irvine, John Campbell, Bob Donahue and John Reason, each of whom furnished opinions, some flattering, some decidedly not, which they personally felt genuinely reflected Scotland's Grand Slam and the reactions to it.

When England won the World Cup in 1966 in the realm of Association Football there were discordant voices, not least from North of the Border, and, as a Scot, one was well aware that not everyone saw Scotland's Grand Slam quite as we did ourselves.

No one and least of all Jim Telfer and his troops would claim that the Scotland XV in 1984 were above criticism and obviously there are times when more can be learned from detractors than from mere hymns of praise. Nevertheless, my own view remains that Scotland's triumphant quadrilateral will stand four-square against the years and deservedly so.

Scotland's first Grand Slam, in 1925, also has an honoured place in these pages, the average age of that side being, according to the Scottish Rugby Union's historian, Sandy Thorburn, just 23.8 by comparison with the 28 of Jim Aitken's team; the only player from a Border club the inimitable Doug Davies as against the eleven who shared in the Grand Slam defeat of France; and among the 77 points they totalled not a single penalty goal in contrast to the ten kicked by Peter Dods as he set in 1984 a new Championship points record for a Scot with his haul of exactly 50.

His distinguished predecessor, Andy Irvine, provides a Foreword and the slant of one so intimately involved in the evolution of the Grand Slam team makes revealing reading.

NORMAN MAIR

Edinburgh, October 1984

Foreword

by Andy Irvine

The Grand Slam is a dream come true for thousands of Scottish rugby enthusiasts, a particular treat for those who have been around a long time, those in their forties, fifties and sixties . . . So many times in the years leading up to 1984 had Scotland been the bridesmaid and I suspect that because we are only a small nation the whole thing has meant that much more, been that bit sweeter. It has also meant more recognition for the game North of the Border. There is greater interest in rugby, far more attention from the media – and this, I feel, is something which could lead to rugby in Scotland attracting more young players.

In the last ten years or so, the number of other things boys can do at school has proliferated. With so many other options open to youngsters, some of rugby's traditionally strong catchment areas have not had the numbers coming through that they used to. My fondest hope is that the winning of the Triple Crown and Grand Slam will rekindle the flame.

Having been lucky enough to be part of the team for so long and yet missed out on this year of years, I greatly welcome the opportunity, afforded by this foreword, to salute not only the collective achievement but individuals.

Jim Aitken has surely provided the right inspiration as captain. He is a chap I have never experienced in that role but he has certainly been a real pack leader in many a game in which we have both played. I have always had a high regard for him in that capacity. He is very good at organizing things on the field and cajoling players, tending to get the best out of them of which they are capable. It is difficult to put a finger on quite what makes players follow one man and not another, but undoubtedly Aitken has that certain knack while no one with any pretence of being fair can deny that his record speaks for itself.

Having said that, I should have to confess that an even more important member of the pack, if not the team, was Iain Milne, simply because as such a huge, strong chap he provided the cornerstone. If anyone doubts the size of his contribution I just ask them to take another look at what happened against Rumania when he was not there.

It is all conjecture now but I still believe that if Iain Milne had played in Bucharest, Scotland could well have won because, by all accounts and the impression one got on television, it was in the scrummage that Scotland lost a crucial measure of control. Again, a lot of the players confirm that a vital factor in the French match was that Iain Milne had his opponents' front row on toast in the closing quarter of an hour.

Colin Deans, with his exceptional mobility allied to his hooking, has never been less than a tremendous asset though Milne, I am sure, has often made a deal of difference to him. What is more, the kind of platform a substantial tight-head of Milne's calibre establishes can transform the lot of the back row, not least in terms of the confidence with which they launch their various ploys.

As regards the second row, there were maybe no great stars, although Alister Campbell looked a grand player in the making. Alan Tomes and Bill Cuthbertson used their experience well and, over the season, were great workhorses. Though they might be the first to admit that they are not world-beaters, they could fairly claim to have done their share towards the season's honours. Cuthbertson, until he had to pull out through injury, could hardly have worn his years more lightly.

Crucially, there was abundant class in the back row. David Leslie, as everyone – or almost everyone – now acknowledges, was the outstanding player in Europe over the season and it is particularly gratifying that having missed out on the Lions' last three tours, through a combination of injury and woeful selection, he was part and parcel of Scotland's finest hours for many a decade. Jim Calder had a magnificent year – and provided the perfect foil to Leslie. Iain Paxton, who cannot have had much to spare in edging out John Beattie in the first place, proceeded to have a great season in a back row which played some unforgettable rugby and which, in combination with the half-backs, frequently controlled the whole show.

Roy Laidlaw and John Rutherford are, of course, now both vastly experienced, having been around a long time at the top. Make no mistake, they can play the wide, expansive game when they want or circumstances so dictate. More relevant for most of the season was that both are very good kickers.

Superfine Chocolates are the result of over fifty years of experience with
the finest confectionery. Established on the twin traditions of quality and individuality,
Superfine Chocolates are produced by craftsmen, proud of their product and jealous
of their reputation.

The specially prepared centres are twice drenched in the finest of covering
chocolate to produce an assortment both exquisite and exclusive. Every box of
Superfine Chocolates contain a delightful variety from the selection
offered on this chart.

Although every box leaves our factory in perfect condition, the chocolates can be
affected by atmospheric changes. This may cause a whitish bloom to appear on the
surface although not necessarily affecting the taste. If you are concerned, please
return the box and its contents to us, together with the date and place of purchase
and we will be delighted to investigate the matter.
This guarantee applies to the U.K. only; it does not affect the consumer's statutory rights.

BENDICKS (MAYFAIR) LTD. WINCHESTER, HANTS, ENGLAND

BENDICKS

SUPERFINE CHOCOLATES

Butterscotch

Almond Topped
Creme

Caramel

Nut Crunch

Violet Creme

Coffee Truffle

Cream O'Devon

Ginger

Almond Roch

Walnut Crisp

Hazel Cup

Mint Truffle

Banana Creme

Brazil

Walnut Dessert

Rum Flavour Truffle

Blackcurrant Creme

Nougat

Marzipan

Rose Creme

Pineapple and
Coconut Creme

Butterscotch
Truffle

Coffee and Ginger
Creme

Rum and Orange
Marzipan

Caramel
Marzipan

Walnut Coffee
Creme

Plain Truffl

Rutherford had a superb season with the boot and both he and Laidlaw were sound in defence – a real bonus for half-backs. Laidlaw, in particular, is your little terrier, possibly one of the best tackling scrum-halves of all time, at one moment taking on hulking forwards coming at him head-on and seemingly mere seconds later producing the kind of saving cover tackle that brings a crowd to its feet. One found oneself thrilling for him, as if he had been one's own son, when he scored his two tries against Ireland.

In the centre, Scotland had, above all, great triers: Keith Robertson with a lot of class, David Johnston with a lot of pace and, until he was injured, Euan Kennedy with that sheer physical presence which is one commodity so many of the Scottish back divisions of the recent past have undeniably lacked.

The centres, perhaps, did not get all that many opportunities to run because so much of Scotland's game-plan was based around the kicking of the half-backs. But they chased and harried in pursuit of such kicks not blindly but with real football intelligence and when the opportunity was there to show what they could do, ball in hand, they did their stuff.

The wings, similarly, were not exactly plied with passes but Roger Baird, even if he had no tries to show for it, had a very useful season, with his defence frequently if not uniformly showing up well and he again, with his speed of foot and ball sense, knows more than a thing or two about pressurizing the opposition.

The lucky mascot, Jim Pollock, did nothing much wrong in the championship matches and came through better than many might have imagined from what they had seen of him on lesser occasions. Steve Munro had the pleasure of sharing in the defeat of Wales in Cardiff, which is still something of a collector's item for any Scottish player.

As for Peter Dods, he had, all in all, a particularly good season and was under-estimated by many people. He kicked some vital goals – which, whether one likes it or not, is apt to be 60 to 70 per cent, if not more, of the winning of a modern international – and he rarely made mistakes. He maybe does not attack as much as one would like to see but he did get in some very important tackles. He was so sound over the whole piece that had there been a Lions tour to follow, I believe he would have gone on it.

The squad's team spirit and dedication were absolutely phenomenal. Rugby gets ever harder in terms of the time, commitment and concentration required. The effort forthcoming last season was beyond praise and always there was the example coming from Jim Telfer himself.

David Leslie, Scotland's version of a ground-to-air missile.

Above left Jim Calder, sleeves symbolically rolled up, delves industriously in support of Leslie's on-the-deck possession at Cardiff.
George Herringshaw

Above right Leslie contests the throw-in. *Bob Thomas*

Below Peter Dods, Andy Irvine's successor and a player to whom Irvine pays particular tribute for his contribution to the Grand Slam, clearing on his own line ahead of Michael Kiernan's follow-up tackle. *Bob Thomas*

I have never come across a more dedicated individual. To my mind, Scotland had been knocking at the door for three or four years, ever since Jim Telfer had taken command as coach. The Grand Slam was but the climax to his years of building upon basically the same squad.

Everybody will be waiting to see how Scotland cope next year without him. Funnily enough, I don't think that he will necessarily be a fatal loss, because he has moulded the players into such a team that they really know what they are doing and where they are going. I more than half expect to see Scotland in 1985 bidding hard for another Triple Crown and, possibly, even another Grand Slam.

It would be very wrong of me to fail to mention Colin Telfer, who was Jim's assistant coach, specializing in the back play. Nothing about his part mattered more than the way Colin Telfer related to John Rutherford since, no matter where the captain is but especially when he is in the tight five, the stand-off has to make decisions. It is the pivotal position.

As for the matches, I shall always claim that Scotland won their Triple Crown and Grand Slam with a lot more style than did Ireland when they won their Triple Crown two or three years ago, pleased for them though so many in the game rightly were. Ireland's Triple Crown lay to an inordinate degree with Ollie Campbell's goal-kicking whereas Scotland's was much more an all-round performance.

As I saw it, the Scotland pack were never really outplayed. At worst they were fifty-fifty and almost always they were winning most of the loose ball, thanks to the back row in general and David Leslie in particular.

Though we had routed Wales in Cardiff two years previously, I should put the 1984 victory ahead of that of the 1982 because it was a more controlled display, much less a case merely of everything going almost miraculously right on the day. Moreover, Wales were a better side in 1984 – quite a useful Welsh side in my book.

England at Murrayfield had unusual problems in terms of fitness but even so we did play darned well, with John Rutherford a match-winning figure.

We really crucified Ireland to clinch the Triple Crown. We got just the start we would have wanted on what could have been a nerve-racking occasion. Having the wind with us probably had a lot to do with that. A bit ironic, of course, because Ireland won the toss and deliberately chose to play against the wind but I don't think that we were going to be stopped that day, wind or no wind.

It was a weak Irish side, admittedly, but not as bad as Scotland made them look with those two spectacular tries towards the close, setting the seal on the winning at long last of the Triple Crown.

Before the Grand Slam match, France possibly deserved to be cast as narrow favourites even though they are seldom the same side away from home. Their panache and pace in the earlier matches had been positively frightening and they could hardly have been more quickly into their stride but, having defended heroically for so much of that first half, we won in the end on guts wedded to a possibly superior fitness.

The will to win born under Jim Telfer's driving coaching was very evident in the last ten minutes when Scotland still had the unity and understanding of a settled club side. You could see the French coming apart at the seams and though Jean-Pierre Rives, as captain, did his utmost to muster his troops, I shall go to my grave believing that Scotland had the winning of the match even before Jerome Gallion left the field injured.

I played for ten or eleven years at that kind of level and I may say that, when I came back into the squad last winter, I sensed at once that the confidence of the team was very much more than skin deep. These players really expected to win and that is not something you could always say of Scottish sides of the past; they even reminded me in that respect of the great Welsh teams of the seventies.

To cap it all, Scotland had in Adam Robson just the kind of president the players would have wished to have had as figure-head in such a year – quiet but popular, a gentleman in every respect and a great player in his day. Scotland have had other good presidents over the last ten years but also, alas, one or two who were mediocre, even downright bad.

Not everyone, of course, saw Scotland's Triple Crown and Grand Slam in quite the same light as we did ourselves. Though as a Scot I might feel that he over-reacted, there is no gainsaying the fact that John Reason, as always, has come up with some very valid points.

I shall content myself with saying simply that it is no crime to play to your strengths and the fault lies not with Scotland but with the legislators who have allowed the game to reach the point where, especially in the kind of conditions you are liable to have in Britain, there is an uncomfortable amount of truth in the notion that you have to be an awful long way ahead of the opposition to be able to win your matches with real style.

The chief author of *The Year of the Thistle* is Norman Mair and I can safely say that there is no more respected rugby writer, not just in Scotland but throughout the United Kingdom and even world-wide. When we play the Australians, the South Africans and the New Zealanders, the talk often turns to journalists and I vividly remember the very high opinion that such as the All Blacks had of Norman. What Bill McLaren does for commentating, Norman Mair does for writing.

It helps, of course, that he has played international rugby and that he has coached schoolboys, club players and those who have attained representative level. He has always been very much on the same wavelength as the top players and I wager that such seasoned campaigners as, say, John Rutherford, Jim Renwick and David Leslie would endorse that sentiment.

In many ways I think he has much in common with the late Carwyn James. He can analyse a game as well as anyone I have ever met and, though most of his coaching was done before I came on the scene, I have long had a personal theory that Scottish rugby lost a potentially marvellous coach when journalism claimed Norman Mair for its own.

It adds immeasurably to his writing that he brings to rugby the perspective of one well versed in other games and when I had the good fortune to meet two of the world's leading golfers – first Gary Player and later Jack Nicklaus – I was intrigued to find that they spoke just as highly of him.

O' Flower of Scotland. The Murrayfield terraces ablaze with Lions Rampant as the French match turns Scotland's way.
Dave Stranock

1
Grand Slam

At around four o'clock on the afternoon of 29 October 1983, the odds against a Scotland Grand Slam in 1984 were to be measured upon the scale of space.

The South, admittedly hit by the withdrawal of the Scotland captain, Jim Aitken, who had gone down with influenza, had been demolished at Netherdale by Stu Wilson's All Blacks to the tune of 30–9 with a try-score of 5–0. And that with Peter Dods, Roger Baird, Keith Robertson, John Rutherford, Roy Laidlaw, Colin Deans, Alan Tomes, Iain Paxton, David Leslie and, coming on as a replacement, Alister Campbell in the Borderers' ranks.

The notices, in the language of the theatre, were as blackly funereal as the All Blacks' magnificently sombre strip – once, incidentally, classified by a New Zealander, Wallace Reyburn, as second only to Scotland's among the major rugby nations.

However, as a beautifully evocative piece of research in the *Glasgow Herald* by Allan Massie was to remind us on the morning of the Triple Crown match with Ireland, the last all-conquering Scotland side, the Triple Crown team of 1938, had been not dissimilarly scalded by the critics.

The 1938 season was to be crowned with 'Wilson Shaw's match' but there was the *Scotsman* thundering about his 'incredibly slack' tackling for Glasgow versus Edinburgh. Massie also unearthed such phrases about a team destined to win Scotland's eighth Triple Crown as 'founded more on hope than expectation' and, more dismissive still, 'whose composition has surprised everyone, including possibly the selectors themselves.'

Not, alas, that plenty of condemned Scotland teams have not lived up gruesomely to their advance billing but rather that in 1938 as in 1984 the critics least confounded turned out to be those who recognized what Scotland had going for them rather than what they had not.

In the first place, Scotland in 1984 had by far the best selection committee I have known in an experience of the Scottish camp dating back, as reserve, player or rugby journalist, to the season of 1949–50. For the record, only Bob Munro had not played for Scotland – and he had worn Edinburgh's colours as a prop in his career with Leith Academicals.

Nothing will ever alter my opinion that, on the long path leading to the Grand Slam, the most important date was 17 January 1981, when Scotland lost to France at Parc de Princes in what was Jim Telfer's first match as Scotland's coach.

Scotland took the field that afternoon with, in their back row, three superb support players in Gordon Dickson, John Beattie and Jim Calder but no obvious ball-winner, particularly as Calder was not then the player he has become. What is more, Scotland were, as anticipated, plainly paying too great a price elsewhere for the not unmixed blessings of great height at the line-out.

Where many another selection committee would have dug in stubbornly, Ian MacGregor and Co. at once changed course. David Leslie was recalled to go in and win the ball on the floor and Bill Cuthbertson to be both foil and sweeper to Alan Tomes. Wales were promptly beaten at Murrayfield but more momentous surely was the demonstration that here were selectors more interested in winning matches than in proving themselves right. It might be possible to disagree with them here and there but, once convinced they were on the right lines, the more recent Scottish selection committees have been nothing if not consistent.

The pack which triumphed in Wales were identical to the pack which played against Rumania in 1981. Set that against the season in the Fifties when Scotland got through more than thirty players and duly and deservedly lost every match. In those days the average follower asked to name the Scotland team for the forthcoming championship might sometimes have done well to be 50 per cent correct whereas in the last few seasons most would have got as many as thirteen or fourteen right.

With the winning of the Grand Slam, those cautionary tales from the darker days of the post-war era can soon be consigned to gather dust in the archives. For instance, the story of how, as if harking back wistfully to the days of 'First up, first down', the selectors once picked Doug Keller as the Scotland hooker for a final trial and never mind that he was a flanker, not a hooker, and much more an Australian than a Scot. And, two years later, having confided to the players that they were going for an attacking back division and would need plenty of ball, nominated that doughty Gala prop forward John Fox to strike against England.

In 1984, the Scots were a notably tightly-knit group with only Bill Cuthbertson, Jim Pollock and Rob Cunningham, among the players and replacements, playing for clubs outside Scotland. Yet, Ian MacGregor, the convener of the selectors, had had to play himself into the Scotland XV in an era when the selectors had been prepared to stretch the qualifications so elastically that cartoonists depicted natives in grass skirts with spears and eskimos with harpoons queuing up for a national trial at Murrayfield. One wag even suggested that Scotland borrow from the nomenclature of Rugby League and dub the teams in the trial Scotland v Other Nationalities, the nadir being reached when a prop, a schoolmaster from the English Midlands, was selected for a national trial and replied that he was English, not Scottish, and would not have come anyway because the match was on the same day as his school play.

Verily, the players of 1984 could count their blessings. The squad system, of course, helps in that, almost by definition, it fosters a settled side. Indeed, given such sessions in the Fifties, the dafter excesses of the selectors might well have been avoided.

''Tis not in mortals to command success but we'll do more Sempronius, we'll deserve it.' There may have been more talented Scottish XVs than that of 1984 but none which worked harder. They gave their all to Telfer, many having come up with him through the B team. By the time they assembled on the Thursday before the Irish match, they had already determinedly fitted in one Sunday and two mid-week squad sessions since their Calcutta Cup victory less than a month before. The mid-week stints were a sensible innovation on the part of the selectors, being popular with the players, who found that they were apt to be shorter but sharper than those on a Sunday and interfered much less with family life and domestic bliss.

For all too long the great weakness of Scottish rugby was the gulf between the club game and the international arena, something the Inter-District Championship and then, twenty years later, the official leagues were introduced to combat.

One used to argue that the leagues in Scotland should not be judged until their second decade because you could not play one way for a hundred years and more, change the structure drastically and expect success overnight. In the eleventh season of the leagues, right on cue, came the Triple Crown and Grand Slam. Though I think that the leagues greatly helped, and that Scotland would probably still not have won the Triple Crown, let alone the Grand

Slam, without their advent, I do not doubt that the experience gained on overseas tours has been a yet more decisive factor. Trips were made to France in 1980, New Zealand in 1981 and Australia in 1982, with Jim Telfer the coach each time, and Ian MacGregor the manager in France and Australia. In addition, eight of those who played in the course of the Grand Slam had been with the 1983 Lions to New Zealand under Telfer while Alan Tomes and John Beattie were Lions in South Africa in 1980.

The players complain, with considerable justification, that many of their club matches are too one-sided or of too low a standard to be of much value, particularly since the ludicrous change from twelve-club divisions to those of fourteen. Nonetheless, by past Scottish standards, this was a uniquely seasoned and battle-hardened task-force well used to the international tempo.

With so much experience on tap it made all the more sense that the players had a far greater say in terms of strategy and tactics than had once been the case. It was on Scotland's 1981 tour of New Zealand that Telfer first learned that the All Blacks coach during team-talks would call upon selected players to go over, for their own benefit and that of the others, how they saw their role in the context of the approaching match in the light of what was known of the enemy. Telfer saw the advantages and adopted the practice at Scotland's Friday evening team-talks. 'I found it helped them and it helped me,' said Telfer.

No one, obviously, was more aware than Jim Telfer that the All Blacks, with whom Scotland drew so dramatically in November, were some way from the All Blacks the Lions had faced in New Zealand. He was equally quick to concede that Wales and England were at something of a transitional stage, although that, as he would murmur sardonically, was hardly Scotland's fault.

He did feel, though, that some of the allegations of negative rugby were less than fair on the players, who, in winning the Triple Crown, scored nine tries – only one fewer than the 1938 side had garnered at a time when defences were less meticulously drilled than they are today. The 1984 side's Grand Slam tally of ten tries was the most by Scotland in the championship for thirty-nine seasons. They conceded only three. Those twin statistics in Telfer's climactic championship should be seen against the background to which he made his debut as national coach.

In the three previous seasons Scotland had drawn once with England and lost to them twice; lost three times to Wales; drawn once with Ireland and lost to them twice; and lost twice to France but beaten them once. In addition, there had been two defeats at

Above The detonator. The captain's winning try in Cardiff from which all else ultimately stemmed. *George Herringshaw*

Below The Grand Slamming smile. Scotland's coach, Jim Telfer (left) with the captain, Jim Aitken, after the climactic triumph at the expense of France. *Bob Thomas*

Murrayfield at the hands of the All Blacks. Scotland had played some lovely running rugby, dashingly adventurous, but – sadly for their coach, Nairn MacEwan – all too often in a lost cause. A Triple Crown, a Grand Slam and a try-score of 10–3? Mon, you must be havering . . .

The first thing Telfer had to do was to get to work on the defence. Those who had shuddered at the looseness of much of the Scottish tackling found comfort in the inference to be drawn from the best of all anecdotes reflecting Telfer's engagingly dour humour: the story of how, when an aspiring coach proudly showed him the innumerable moves his team had for kick-offs, Telfer merely grunted, 'I dinna much like sides which kick off more than once.'

Nairn MacEwan, as a player, had been justly famed for his constructive leading out from the mauls and broken play and it inevitably influenced his thinking as a coach. Telfer, in contrast, was a great advocate of the ruck, particularly for Scottish forwards who, he considered, often lacked the necessary upper-body strength for the maul but who could be taught to hit the rucks in unison, low and hard and 'spine-in-line', as the New Zealanders say.

In Scotland at least, he will be judged in retrospect largely by his Grand Slam side and he would be the first to say that they very definitely played to their strengths rather than to please.

The way Scotland mostly used relatively short lines of communication, pressurized their opponents and played much of their game through their back row and halves was surely not so very different from the tactics favoured in 1979 by the North of England when they defeated the All Blacks 21–9. Yet remember the almost unqualified praise heaped upon the North's historic victory. Nevertheless, one has much sympathy for those who worry that we are uncomfortably close to those stifled days, before such changes as the hindmost foot off-side law, the ten-metres-back line-out restriction and the Australian dispensation, when players too often saw the most attractive and the most effective way to play as being poles apart.

It is still possible to play some searing attacking rugby behind the scrum – as the Wallabies, All Blacks, Tricolors and Springboks have all painfully reminded opposition from these islands in the recent past. But those who look back to the great year of 1971 when Carwyn James and his Lions had their unforgettable triumph in New Zealand and Wales won that Alfred Hitchcock thriller at Murrayfield – Alun Williams remarking devoutly that never again would 19–18 connote to him the Great War – should appreciate the effect the subsequent introduction of that one-metre mandatory spacing at the line-out has had on back-play.

It is not yet, of course, back to the bad old days when the line-out stretched far infield with two centres bristling in offensive-defence virtually as an extension of it. The point is, though, that the compressed line-outs of around 1971 produced at once the most illegal but the most usable ball in the whole history of the line-out whereas now, once again, the breakaways are able to take aim on the enemy midfield.

The chain reaction in terms of pressure was caught perfectly in a conversational exchange with the elusive, light-footed thorough-bred that was Gerald Davies in his rugby days. 'Before the coming of the one-metre spacing between players of the same side, I used to reckon that, all other things being equal, I had a seventy-five per cent chance of beating my opposite number. Once the spacing was introduced, I should say it dropped to about forty per cent.'

That stated, it will be intriguing to see if the Grand Slam inspires this Scotland side to expand their game by erasing the remaining traces of the inferiority complex which haunted Scottish rugby after the 44-0 drubbing from South Africa at Murrayfield in 1951. When that match kicked off on 24 November 1951 Scotland, in terms of encounters won and lost, trailed England by only 29–27 and Wales by 27–26 and led Ireland and France by, respectively, 34–25 and 14–6. Today England lead Scotland by 47 wins to 37, and Wales are ahead by 49 to 37. Scotland's advantage over Ireland has shrunk to 47–43 and they are level with France at 26–26.

That is for the future but in the meantime Scottish rugby savours hungrily a Grand Slam which, perhaps excusably after fifty-nine barren years, did not brush even lightly across the mind of any of the panel of experts analysing on radio the prospects for the 1984 Five Nations Championship.

The panel had inclined towards France as the likely champions with England as runners-up and the best listening Scots could take out of it was their enjoyment of Barry John's parting sally. Barry had gone, albeit a little reluctantly, not for France but for England on the score of their forward strength. An Englishman on the panel, in mock disbelief, exclaimed: 'Would you just say that again, Barry?'

'No,' retorted Barry. 'It was hard enough to say it once!'

2
Leslie's Match

WALES (9) v SCOTLAND (15)
Played at Cardiff, 21 January 1984

WALES		SCOTLAND
15 H. Davies (Bridgend)	*Full-back*	15 P. W. Dods (Gala)
14 M. H. Titley (Bridgend)	*Right wing*	14 S. Munro (Ayr)
13 R. A. Ackerman (London Welsh)	*Centre*	13 D. I. Johnston (Watsonians)
12 B. Bowen (South Wales Police)	*Centre*	12 A. E. Kennedy (Watsonians)
11 A. M. Hadley (Cardiff)	*Left wing*	11 G. R. T. Baird (Kelso)
10 M. Dacey (Swansea)	*Stand-off*	10 J. Y. Rutherford (Selkirk)
9 M. H. J. Douglas (Llanelli)	*Scrum-half*	9 R. J. Laidlaw (Jedforest)
1 S. T. Jones (Pontypool)	*Loose-head prop*	1 J. Aitken (**captain**) (Gala)
2 W. J. James (Aberavon)	*Hooker*	2 C. T. Deans (Hawick)
3 R. Morgan (Newport)	*Tight-head prop*	3 I. G. Milne (Heriot's FP)
4 S. J. Perkins (Pontypool)	*Lock*	4 W. Cuthbertson (Harlequins)
5 R. L. Norster (Cardiff)	*Lock*	5 A. J. Tomes (Hawick)
6 R. D. Moriarty (Swansea)	*Flanker*	6 J. H. Calder (Stewart's Melville FP)
7 D. F. Pickering (Llanelli)	*Flanker*	7 D. G. Leslie (Gala)
8 E. T. Butler (**captain**) (Pontypool)	*No. 8*	8 I. A. M. Paxton (Selkirk)

REPLACEMENTS
16 G. Evans (Maesteg)
17 D. S. Richards (Swansea)
18 R. Giles (Aberavon)
19 M. Watkins (Newport)
20 I. Stephens (Bridgend)
21 M. Brown (Pontypool)

REPLACEMENTS
16 N. A. Rowan (Boroughmuir)
17 R. Cunningham (Bath)
18 J. R. Beattie (Glasgow Acads)
19 I. G. Hunter (Selkirk)
20 K. W. Robertson (Melrose)
21 D. S. Wyllie (Stewart's Melville FP)

Referee O. Doyle; touch judges D. H. Burnett and J. R. West (Ireland)

Before the match all Wales and much of Scotland expected Wales to run it wide but by kick-off, Jim Telfer, whose tactical anticipation was one of the outstanding features of the season, had come round to the view that, in the event, Wales would play much of it close and down the narrow side.

Two years before, when Scotland had trounced Wales 34–18 with a try score of five–one, there had been sundry costly Welsh mistakes in the face of the withering speed of the Scottish midfield offensive-defence. So often the reaction to such mistakes is that the victims take the field at the next time of asking determined to minimize the risk of forced and unforced errors and to endeavour to make more room for themselves behind the scrum by initially taking the foe on up front.

Even if all this did not prove a factor, or only a subconscious one, it always seemed likely that a scrum-half of Mark Douglas's type would frequently be tempted into using his strength down the blind-side while the fact that Wales had picked, with the inclusion of Richard Moriarty at flank forward, four big men was an added inducement to Douglas to play back to his forwards.

With Scotland rucking splendidly, a vintage David Leslie winning virtually everything at the tail of the line-out and Scotland hell-bent on pressurizing everywhere, Wales did not have all that much of the brand of ball which simply begs to be run. Those pre-match prophesies, voiced so strongly in so many quarters, that Wales would constantly be shipping it wide duly came to grief as Telfer had foreseen.

The national trial, which had brought so many of the Scotland players rudely back to earth after the heady drama of the 25–25 draw with the All Blacks, had seen the Whites defeating the senior side by 21–3 and four tries to nil. Steve Munro, Euan Kennedy, who had missed the trial with a virus infection, Roy Laidlaw, Alan Tomes, Iain Paxton and David Leslie came back at the expense of, respectively, Jim Pollock, Jim Renwick, Gordon Hunter, Tom Smith, John Beattie and John Jeffrey. In retrospect, at the other end of the Grand Slam, the idea of Scotland without Laidlaw and Leslie seemed bizarre indeed.

Only four Welsh players had survived from the side routed in Cardiff by Scotland in 1982 – Robert Ackerman, Robert Norster, Richard Moriarty and Eddie Butler – and the difference in experience, statistically at least, was spectacular. Wales had three new caps in Howell Davies, Mark Douglas and Rhys Morgan, Ian Eidman's late replacement, while Scotland had none. Five of the Welsh backs had never previously played in a match in the International Championship and whereas Scotland had amassed 266 caps, Wales totalled only 60. More remarkable still was a point singled out by Bill Lothian of the *Edinburgh Evening News*: that Scotland actually had more than twice as many British Lions in their side as had Wales.

The new South stand at the Welsh National Stadium restricts the amount of light on the pitch and, as a precaution against frost, the field had been covered with polythene sheeting. The surface was a little softer than the head groundsman, Bill Hardiman, would perhaps have wanted. As is his habit on winning the toss, Jim Aitken chose to take what wind there was.

With half an hour gone, Scotland were penalized for going over the top as they contested the ball on the ground at the rear of a line-out and Davies kicked a fine goal. In injury-time in the first half, Wales were penalized, in the person of Eddie Butler, for having three men in the line-out when Scotland, whose throw it was and who could therefore dictate the number, had only two. Colin Deans took the tap free-kick and passed left to Laidlaw. Deans came round as a decoy on a dummy run as Laidlaw instead fed the ball back right to Rutherford: the stand-off broke for Leslie to erupt on to his pass and give to Iain Paxton who sped clear off the pursuing Moriarty and dived over, not deliberately flamboyantly but because he knew not who was behind him.

The last two passes, from Rutherford to Leslie and from Leslie to Paxton, looked suspiciously forward and one English scribe observed that it reminded him of baton-changing. But there were not many complaints from the Welsh, so much had that footballing nation found to admire in the conception and execution.

The goal Peter Dods kicked to bring up his fifty points for his country concluded the first half, giving Scotland a 6–3 lead which was a disappointing return for their share of the play.

An hour of the match had passed before Wales scored from a set scrum close to the Scottish line after the promising Adrian Hadley had come stirringly into the attack far out on the right from the left wing. Butler picked up and gave to Douglas who beat Jim Calder on the outside. The powerful scrum-half committed Roger Baird before putting the ball back inside to the scissoring Mark Titley for the wing to score his first try for Wales as Roy Laidlaw tackled despairingly.

There was a period when Scotland leaked try after try down a left-hand blind-side from set scrums on the opposition's ball. Jim Calder, in such circumstances, has long been prepared to break early and stand off the scrum, normally to great effect. At Cardiff,

Above Though giving away five inches, David Leslie brings his greater experience of the tail-gunner's role to bear as he once more loses Richard Moriarty in the jump. *Bob Thomas*

Below Crash landing. Iain Paxton at the completion of his spectacular dive in the scoring of Scotland's first try in the defeat of Wales. *George Herringshaw*

though, he broke off too wide, giving the man with the ball two ways to go, the choice of attacking him on his inside or outside.

Possibly because of an uncertainty born of that very positioning, Calder tended rather to wait on his man instead of going in to meet him with more momentum. The other point, of course, is that if you hang back and the tackle misses, the defence, particularly when so close to the line, is caught fatally flat. If you advance to get in the tackle that little bit earlier there is at least that much more chance of cover getting in behind you.

Davies kicked a lovely goal but, within three minutes, Scotland were level as Douglas was penalized for coming round off-side at a set scrum. And then, with twelve minutes to go, Deans yet again found Leslie with a long throw to the tail. Calder took the deflection supported by Paxton and Bill Cuthbertson and, as the ball came back, Laidlaw wheeled to link with John Rutherford who chipped through, the thrust ending with Deans in touch just short of the Welsh line.

Billy James's throw was to the middle of the line-out and it spilled to Iain Milne who rumbled massively for the line. As he was checked but possession retained, Laidlaw sniped for the try but he too was thwarted. Once more – and nothing could have been more typical of this Scotland side – the ball was kept available, Aitken picking up and plunging over through the tackle of Douglas with the inevitable Leslie thudding into his captain's buttocks in driving support.

Dods kicked the goal despite his boot having split. Emergency repairs at half-time having failed, Dods kicked those priceless second-half goals with his stockinged toes taking the air. It spoke volumes for his temperament, though it obviously helped that he is an instep-kicker rather than a toe-kicker, while the party piece of Bob Scott, the great New Zealand full-back, used to be to kick goals from the half-way line in his bare feet.

Frantically, Wales strove to save the game but the Scottish defence held out, the match ending with the ball escaping Douglas's grasp once again on the blind-side of a scrum threateningly close to the Scottish line.

Never before had Scotland won twice in three seasons in Cardiff and, indeed, prior to 1982 they had triumphed there only three times in fifty-seven years. David Leslie's Match, as it was christened after the match-winning display by the Scotland tail-gunner, was already bound for the record books long before it transpired that it was the first leg of a Grand Slam.

Above Roy Laidlaw, whose heroic covering was frequently worth an extra flanker to Scotland's already formidable back row, is just too late to deny Mark Titley the trenchantly-worked and cleverly-taken Welsh try. *George Herringshaw*

Below Jim Aitken's try gives Scotland back the lead with Iain Paxton kneeling in grateful homage. *Bob Thomas*

Wales had announced their team after Scotland named theirs but, interestingly, Jim Telfer confirmed that the Scottish selection would have remained exactly the same even if they had known that Wales would pick Moriarty at blind-side flank forward and therefore have four pretty big men to compete at the line-out. Behind that assertion lay Telfer's conviction that, against such a Welsh line-out array, Scotland would be more than compensated for any disadvantage in height by being far better equipped to win the ball on the floor. They proceeded to prove him decisively right with Leslie emphasizing his reputation as the best ball-winner on the deck in the championship.

Furthermore, with the aid of the uncannily accurate and perceptive throwing of Deans, to whom he afterwards paid generous tribute, Leslie destroyed Moriarty at the back of the line-out, even beating him on occasion to the Welsh throw.

Leslie always cites Gordon Strachan, the former Scotland back-row forward, and the world of American football as his main sources of inspiration in the specialized business of playing off the back of the line-out.

'Gordon Strachan was a basketball player,' he explains, 'and I saw how he would bring his basketball skills into play by taking the longer throw on the move. Again, not only have I picked up something from American football about pressurizing opponents but there is much to be learned from their receivers when it comes to beating the opposition to a torpedo throw.' Considering he was giving away four inches to Moriarty, his display was one for the connoisseur.

The decision of the Welsh selectors to retain Moriarty in the No. 6 jersey after what had happened against Scotland amazed much of the rugby world. It would have been less of a surprise to those who had heard the Welsh coach, John Bevan, spiritedly defend his performance against Scotland.

In fact, Bevan, a greatly respected figure among the Welsh cognoscenti, went so far as to put Moriarty's defence of the blind-side on the day far ahead of that of Jim Calder. The Scot after all, Bevan added, had been playing on the flank for ten years or more whereas Moriarty was but newly come to the berth from lock and No. 8.

To many, Moriarty's defence of the blind-side had been the least of it. His inability to find an answer to the work of the Scottish back row on the ground and his difficulties at the line-out, to which aspect of play he chiefly owed his selection, mattered far more.

Apart from the fact that you hardly needed to be a Sherlock Holmes to catch this Moriarty in the act, so blatant were his moments of indiscipline, this not untalented fellow looked miserably miscast as the end man in the line-out.

'It was daft,' opined the great Mervyn Davies. 'I should have been almost as uncomfortable in that role myself. Second from the end is one thing but right at the back is a completely different ball game, not least because of all the space behind you.' Time and again, the unfortunate Moriarty simply did not know where Leslie was or where he was coming from, which did much to render his advantage in height null and void.

Years ago, long before it was fashionable, Herbert Waddell used to want the ball thrown to the back to commit the enemy breakaways. Thus, a further disadvantage of the Welsh line-out stationing was that, with Moriarty positioned at the very rear, their fast man, Dave Pickering, was embroiled farther up the line-out. Suffice to say that Wales did not make the same mistake in any of their subsequent matches, for which Moriarty and Pickering must have been equally grateful.

'True grit,' was Jim Aitken's summation of Scotland's hard won victory, a match he deemed physically tougher than the game with the All Blacks. Jim Telfer, who had had several of the Welsh players under him with the Lions in New Zealand, spoke of the 'total commitment' of both sides. In an abrasive, bruising match that commitment at times had overstepped the mark. Owen Doyle, on his debut as an international referee, speaking words of warning once to John Perkins and twice to Moriarty.

Behind the scrum John Rutherford was sometimes uncharacteristically hesitant, twice declining the kind of gap for which he thirsts and twice failing to add from inviting opportunities to the seven goals he had already dropped for Scotland, two of them in the previous international against the All Blacks. Nonetheless, it was a measure of how good a player he has become and the depth of his experience that he rode his troubles, providing, among other telling contributions, the vital incision that led to Paxton's try and the probing little punt which brought the line-out from which his captain, Jim Aitken, was to score the winning try.

Roger Baird was badly beaten early on by Mark Titley, which is not something which has often happened to the erstwhile Scottish Schools scrum-half since he learned the angles involved in his senior berth of wing three-quarter. Whether it was merely a one-off incident or Titley really had the beating of Baird remained unresolved because, where so many of the backs of yesteryear would

Above Scotland's beautifully integrated back row captured in characteristic action with Jim Calder driving off the arch ball-winner, David Leslie, and Iain Paxton driving on Calder. *George Herringshaw*

Below An early skirmish at Cardiff and Jim Aitken in the warm, not to say heated, embrace of Robert Norster. *Alan Macdonald*

have taken it as a signal to ply Titley, the Welsh seemed to have all manner of other things they wanted to do with the ball.

Baird did have his better moments if nothing quite to rival that never-to-be-forgotten run out of defence which set Scotland on their way in 1982. David Johnston and Euan Kennedy tackled trenchantly, with one tackle by Kennedy on Ackerman vying in value with a tackle much later in the game by Dods on Titley.

Leslie's heroics at the line-out offset the shortage of ball from the middle of the line-out, where Wales had Norster, but otherwise the forwards went well with Calder and Paxton forming with the brilliant Leslie a consistently effective and beautifully balanced back row.

Paxton's industry had been thought to make for a better blend than the more mercurial and explosive talents of John Beattie. He had a very good match, taking his try admirably and deserving marks for getting up in support of a lightning break by Laidlaw though, alas, he could not hold on to what was by no means the easiest of passes with the Welsh defence gaping wide.

In his sweeping support of David Leslie at the tail of the line-out, Calder was nothing less than immense. There was, too, one ball late in the game and deep in Scottish territory which broke awkwardly at the front of the line-out but on to which Deans fastened in a flash. Almost in the same instant, he had Calder's driving support at his shoulder, one of those unconsidered little things which can protect possession and make all the difference between victory and defeat in a tight match.

It is held in Wales that one of the reasons that the attractive stand-off that is Malcolm Dacey took his time to exude the authority you look for in an international stand-off was that, in the Swansea midfield, it is Dave Richards who calls the shots. Be that as it may, this looked the kind of defeat from which a side could learn much and, with such as Dacey, Bleddyn Bowen, Mark Titley and Adrian Hadley giving some exciting glimpses of what they could do, one left Cardiff grateful that Scotland had caught this transitional Welsh side so early in the championship.

How many tries, Aitken was asked afterwards, had he scored in his career? 'One or two,' he shrugged, airily.

'Well, which?' inquired a heartless humorist, Aitken joining in the laughter.

THROUGH WELSH EYES

Clem Thomas with John Bevan

In no other corner of the British Isles has rugby football been embraced so emphatically as in Wales. It has become the national game, a way of life, snarled up with their other loves, religion and politics. It is understandable therefore that Welshmen have a burning ambition to win, to be the best, and after a century they can statistically indulge in the conceit that they have won more games than they have lost against the other teams in the Five Nations Championship.

To be patronizing is not a Welsh trait, they are more likely to be uncompromisingly combative, believing that expectation of victory is part of the natural order of their lives. They accept defeat grudgingly and sometimes resentfully.

The Welsh view of Scotland's success in winning the Grand Slam in the season 1983–84 is relevant. It was respectful but qualified. The traumas of those Welsh pilgrimages to a ground which they had ample cause to rename Worryfield and that stunning defeat at Cardiff in 1982 by 34 points to 18, which included five tries, the first storming of the Welsh citadel since the French won in 1968, gave reason for the general Welsh view that a Scottish triumph was long overdue.

There was also evidence that Wales felt that justice had been done. The street-wise rugby public in the Principality had sensed that the Lions tour to New Zealand of 1983 had perpetrated an injustice to the magnificent Jim Telfer and there was considerable delight in the vindication of his reputation.

The Welsh, however, are not the kind to accept such a blow to their own ambitions and aspirations without a prolonged post mortem of their own demise and deficiencies against Scotland or analysing the virtues of Scotland's success.

The consensus of opinion inclined to the view that Scotland's definitive winning of the Grand Slam was largely achieved by their fine morale and spirit. It was also felt that their discipline played a large part, as Scotland gave away fewer penalties than any team in the championship and therefore conceded by far the lowest number of points in the tournament – 36 compared with Wales's 60, France's 67, England's 83 and Ireland's 87. Scotland were also the second highest point scorers with 86 to France's 90.

It was not conceded that Scotland were a particularly great side; while the fallibility of temperament saw the French reverting to their legendary bad habit of losing their cool, a factor to which it must be said that Jean-Pierre Rives, in the twilight of his career, contributed by blighting his capacity for leadership, which was further evidenced by French attitudes against Wales and in New Zealand during the summer. It was the Welsh conviction that in terms of constructive rugby France and Wales were the most exciting teams in the championship, but that neither side played to their potential, and that Wales lost to Scotland in part due to the intransigence and default of their selectors who got it all wrong against Japan, Rumania and Scotland.

Prior to the Scotland game it was obvious to everyone but the Welsh selectors that there were problems on the loose head of the scrum and that therefore the back row was going to be vulnerable on the ground against such well known grovellers as Leslie and Calder. So it proved and the propping of Milne in particular and Aitken and the ground possession from Leslie and Calder proved decisive.

Although Wales recognized Scotland's good fortune in the two seemingly forward passes to Paxton for his try and six points, there was no quibbling about the fact that Wales had not deserved to win.

There is no better man to discuss the match with than the person who coached Wales that day, outside half John Bevan, who because of the presence of Phil Bennett gained only four caps in 1975 and also understudied the maestro on the 1977 Lions tour of New Zealand.

John Bevan took over the coaching of the Welsh side at a difficult time – after the crowning years of the 1970s when Welsh rugby reached a zenith at least in the European context due to an era when the individual genius of a plethora of great players such as Barry John, Phil Bennett, Gareth Edwards, Gerald Davies, John Dawes, J. P. R. Williams and Mervyn Davies expressed themselves within the first genuine squad and coaching system applied in the northern hemisphere. Unhappily the conveyor belt which had churned out great stars suddenly stopped, Welsh club rugby declined and the Welsh team became mortal and vulnerable.

Bevan was a forthright thinking player and he has established the same reputation as a coach. He believes fundamentally in the expansive game and when I asked him what the Welsh tactics were against Jim Aitken's team he told me:

'There were no set tactics against Scotland. While we were fully aware of the well known Scottish capacity to prey on mistakes, we were still determined to go on the field intent to play expansive fifteen-man rugby and to adjust to the opposition. In the event we had difficulties in the front five, we had severe problems in the front row and Scotland recognizing the danger of Bob Norster, disrupted him. Deans threw to Leslie running backwards at the tail of the line-out and Moriarty failed to read it.

'We never envisaged Deans and Leslie using that ploy in the line-out. We should have changed our strategy and put Pickering as rear gunner on the tail as he was much more experienced at playing off the end of the line. Moriarty who plays mainly as lock for his club, Swansea, was used to jumping only on his own ground, and once the ball went over him he was lost. It was a major mistake on our part and it had an immense effect on the game. Scotland disrupted us brilliantly in these areas and subsequently we were in no position throughout the game to develop our attacks.

'Scotland made the most of all their opportunities, even though Rutherford who is such a clever and experienced player took a lot of wrong options. Apart from the deficiencies of the Welsh team on the day, we did not make many mistakes, it was merely that Scotland played to their strength and took their opportunities by playing to them. I gave them ten out of ten for their magnificent achievement of winning at Cardiff.'

When I asked Bevan what he considered were Scotland's strengths, he replied: 'They had a superb middle five, by this I mean the back row of David Leslie, Jim Calder and Iain Paxton and the half-backs, Roy Laidlaw and John Rutherford. They outplayed us in the line-outs and the rucks and although I thought there was a great deal of illegal play on the ground, they certainly got to broken play far faster and got the ball away. It was the fact that they handled so well off the ground that there were so few rucks, which was a disadvantage to us as we expected to beat them in that phase of play.

'In terms of individual play, apart from the middle five, I was impressed by Iain Milne who proved so destructive in the scrums and the way in which Tomes, Cuthbertson and Leslie disrupted our line-outs. Colin Deans was splendid not only for his throwing in at the line-out but for his all-round ability. I am baffled why he never played in a Test in New Zealand. Another Scottish player who surprised us was Peter Dods: he played so much better than we thought he could play and our kicking to him proved fruitless and counterproductive.'

On the question of the excessive use of the blind side by Wales, he claimed: 'The Welsh backs were inexperienced and playing Mark Douglas at scrum-half was an attempt to emulate the strength of Terry Holmes around the base of the forwards. He probes fiercely around the base but on the day he overdid the narrow side and carried Malcolm Dacey with him.'

On the subject of the referee and the Welsh charges of illegal play on the ground and the crucial try by Paxton, Bevan was charitable: 'Owen Doyle enjoys our confidence, he is not in our view the archetypal blind Irish referee, he missed a few things on the day but as I have already said we were outplayed at the line-out and in the loose.

'We were never influenced by that catastrophic Scottish win two years previously. We felt confident that lightning would not strike twice in the same place and certainly not in our own national stadium, we were convinced we were going to win and I still believe it was a game we should have won but we only had ourselves to blame.'

Perhaps the most pertinent comment by John Bevan was his reference to the lack of experience. Only two Welsh players ran into double figures, Eddie Butler the captain and number eight with 12, and Robert Ackerman, the centre, with 13.

Nevertheless most Welshmen stick with the view that their selectors carried the responsibility of blame for choosing a team which found little public support when it was announced. It was a far different side once they gave the captaincy to Mike Watkins and introduced Ian Stephens at loose head and after, essentially, the return of Holmes following the injury sustained in New Zealand. Once the front five were properly assembled, it became a far better team and although for the rest of the season they kept the back row which was beaten out of sight by Scotland, they were never again tested in defence.

The feeling persists that if the same back row plays in Edinburgh next season, they could again prove a Welsh Achilles' heel against that familiar Scottish swashbuckling, which is as good a way of winning a Grand Slam as any.

3

Hare Hunting

SCOTLAND (18) v ENGLAND (6)
Played at Murrayfield, 4 February 1984

SCOTLAND		ENGLAND
15 P. W. Dods (Gala)	*Full-back*	15 W. H. Hare (Leicester)
14 K. W. Robertson (Melrose)	*Right wing*	14 J. Carleton (Orrell)
13 A. E. Kennedy (Watsonians)	*Centre*	13 G. H. Davies (Wasps)
12 D. I. Johnston (Watsonians)	*Centre*	12 C. R. Woodward (Leicester)
11 G. R. T. Baird (Kelso)	*Left wing*	11 M. A. C. Slemen (Liverpool)
10 J. Y. Rutherford (Selkirk)	*Stand-off*	10 L. Cusworth (Leicester)
9 R. J. Laidlaw (Jedforest)	*Scrum-half*	9 N. G. Youngs (Leicester)
1 J. Aitken (captain) (Gala)	*Loose-head prop*	1 C. White (Gosforth)
2 C. T. Deans (Hawick)	*Hooker*	2 P. J. Wheeler (captain) (Leicester)
3 I. G. Milne (Heriot's FP)	*Tight-head prop*	3 G. S. Pearce (N'ampton)
4 W. Cuthbertson (Harlequins)	*Lock*	4 M. J. Colclough (Wasps)
5 A. J. Tomes (Hawick)	*Lock*	5 S. Bainbridge (Gosforth)
6 J. H. Calder (Stewart's Melville FP)	*Flanker*	6 P. D. Simpson (Bath)
7 D. G. Leslie (Gala)	*Flanker*	7 P. J. Winterbottom (Headingley)
8 I. A. M. Paxton (Selkirk)	*No. 8*	8 J. P. Scott (Cardiff)

REPLACEMENTS
16 N. A. Rowan (Boroughmuir)
17 R. Cunningham (Bath)
18 J. R. Beattie (Glasgow Acads)
19 I. G. Hunter (Selkirk)
20 D. S. Wyllie (Stewart's Melville FP)
21 J. A. Pollock (Gosforth)

REPLACEMENTS
16 N. C. Stringer (Wasps)
17 B. Barley (Wakefield)
18 R. Hill (Bath)
19 P. J. Blakeway (Gloucester)
20 S. G. B. Mills (Gloucester)
21 J. Hall (Bath)

Referee D. I. H. Burnett; touch judges O. E. Doyle and J. R. West (Ireland)

The team talk that held the key to Scotland's winning of the ninety-first Calcutta Cup and their hundredth international against England came late on the morning of the match.

The most painstaking of coaches, Jim Telfer is renowned for his attention to detail, which goes right down to the condition and length of the last stud, and on the morning of an international he invariably goes to the ground to get the feel of the likely conditions. That day, he had particularly wished to find out how the new East stand would affect the swirl of the wind. He had discovered a relatively quiet patch at the Clock end under the shadow of the new stand and something not dissimilar at the other end.

Yet what mattered more than the wind, which eased a little in any case, was that Telfer came away from SRU headquarters with the image of a wet and slippery ball freshly imprinted on his thinking. A glance or two out of the windows of the team's hotel would not necessarily have had anything like the same impact.

Various pundits had suggested that, on the evidence of their display against the All Blacks, the strength of the England forwards was such that Scotland, by comparison with the Welsh match, would have to open up much more in the way of a second front and attack more often through their backs. Telfer had conceded that the contention was not without a certain logic, though I personally doubt if Scotland were ever likely to have made too much of a radical change in the basic game-plan which had become the norm under the former Melrose international. At any rate, Rutherford has said since that dank February afternoon that, with firm turf and a dry ball, he would have been seeking to swing his centres into action.

But the weather on the day of the match clarified the issue. 'You would not have needed a very high IQ to have worked out how we were going to play,' Telfer had said wryly after the Welsh match, but this time it was a matter of shaping the game-plan to exploit conditions which might have been sent from heaven to allow Scotland to demonstrate the areas in which they were superior to the Sassenachs.

Scotland, as it turned out, scrummaged well enough to have Peter Wheeler, England's captain and famed hooker, acknowledge that England had been under the greater pressure on their own ball, and Scotland even did rather better at the throw-in than many had expected. As Roy Laidlaw put it to a member of the SRU's hierarchy, 'We get all geared up for a superhuman effort in the loose to offset the set-pieces and then have the bonus of finding ourselves doing none too badly in the set-pieces after all.'

Nevertheless, Telfer was to confirm afterwards that he had reckoned it not just prudent but probably realistic to assume that England would mount a more formidable scrummage than the Welsh eight who had played against Scotland, that their middle jumpers would pose even more of a threat, and that, with a trio of authentic back-row forwards, they would be much better organized at the back of the line-out than the Welsh had been and far better too on the deck.

Against all that, Scotland looked the more mobile and manoeuvrable pack, the difference running down the very spine of the scrum from the little tornado, Deans, via the two locks, Cuthbertson and Tomes, to the loping stride of Paxton at No. 8. On such a day the diagonal kick, either lofted or low and skidding, was an obvious and ideal weapon to turn and stretch those heavier-footed English forwards.

To that extent, of course, the choice of kick dictated the kicker, since it is much more a stand-off's kick than a scrum-half's. But Laidlaw's inquisitive chips down the short side were complementary to the searching punts which John Rutherford, playing throughout with an authority which was uniform where it had been a little fitful in the Welsh match, added to much first-rate defensive clearing.

The other great advantage of the wet ball from Scotland's point of view was that it was patently more likely to suit a rucking pack, such as Scotland's, rather than a mauling one, such as England's. Not only did Scotland take the field sensibly and fiercely determined, so far as the frontal battle was concerned, 'to get the ball on the deck as much as possible', but they made a shrewd and sophisticated modification to their habitual technique. After the establishment of what Telfer terms a mini-ruck, instead of a forward gathering and driving anew as they so often do, Scotland mostly drove over the ball and left the pick-up of that slippery object to the more practised hands of Laidlaw.

Such clearly defined thinking was all in marked contrast to the uncertainty in England's mauling to which, Wheeler agreed, the wet and greasy ball had predictably contributed.

The strong-running Steve Munro, who had missed the All Blacks match because of a leg injury, had gone over on an ankle in training on the Thursday. His cruel misfortune let in that ethereally elusive footballer, Keith Robertson, the expectation being that Robertson's general utility and, in particular, his copybook fielding were likely to be especially valuable on such a day.

Aitken, as one had come to expect, chose to play with the wind on winning the toss. At half-time, Scotland led 6–3, Dusty Hare, with the last act of the half, having landed a penalty goal from forty yards in reply to a try by Johnston in which the dark blue of Scotland was heavily laced with the maroon of Hearts.

The Scottish backs, and most notably the two wings, Keith Robertson and Roger Baird, chased, harried and hounded like beasts of prey in support of Rutherford's diagonals and it was a follow-up tackle by Baird on Hare from a left-footed punt by Rutherford which earned the line-out in the vicinity of the 22-metre line from which Scotland opened the scoring. Leslie got a hand to the long throw from Deans and, as the England centres over-ran the barely deflected stray ball, Paxton got a foot to it. In the kind of situation where, had it been soccer, one would have been glancing anxiously touchwards to see if the linesman's flag was up for off-side, Johnston, with his scalding acceleration and the skills which once excited the old Hearts and Scotland manager, the late Willie Ormond, slipped it past Hare and dived to score a try which Dods safely converted from some fifteen yards in from touch.

Possibly fearful lest anyone think he was making too much of

The speed and soccer skills of David Johnston bring him Scotland's first try in the Calcutta Cup as (left to right) Dusty Hare, Clive Woodward and Les Cusworth are left helpless. *Bob Thomas*

the fact he had once played for Hearts, Johnston was quick to deny that he ever said, 'As they say in football, I controlled it with my right and put it away with my left.' But, of course, great deeds such as the winning of Calcutta Cups, Triple Crowns and Grand Slam engender all manner of apocryphal anecdotes. The fact that Johnston never said it will, I fancy, no more affect the telling and re-telling of such a choice line than did the avowal by a descendant of Queen Victoria who had actually known that imposing lady that the Widow of Windsor had never actually said, 'We are not amused.' The same goes for the tale of how, after being presented to Princess Anne twice in a short space of time, Roy Laidlaw had murmured, 'We really can't go on meeting like this.'

Even before Johnston's try, Cuthbertson had been damaged at the bottom of a ruck, injuring his groin in an involuntary splits enforced by the weight of bodies. In what he was to describe as the hardest decision he had ever made, but fearing that he would be little more than a passenger, he departed at half-time not to return.

It was Cuthbertson who, characteristically, had fastened on to a ricochet in his role of sweeper rather than jumper to provide the line-out ball from which Johnston, taking advantage of Murrayfield's expansive in-goal area, had punted with mathematical precision for Jim Pollock's equalizing try against Stu Wilson's All Blacks. The bearded and embattled, piratical veteran had been an integral part of Jim Telfer's plans since Telfer's second match as Scotland's coach, the windswept defeat of Wales at Murrayfield in 1981. Neither tall nor heavy by the standards applicable to a modern international lock, Cuthbertson has always been best deployed as the foil alongside a much bigger lock with other line-out options also available within the back row. His sweeping at the line-out has always been of the highest class and, for all Cuthbertson's earlier tendency to give away foolish penalties, Telfer, at the end of his own reign as Scotland's coach, paid him a simple and unvarnished tribute: 'To me and for me he has been a great player.'

John Beattie came on as Cuthbertson's replacement, packing down in the second row, a berth with which he was familiar in earlier years. His introduction thereby left the back row undisturbed, one change in this instance very definitely being better than two.

With Scotland's considerable depth of reserves in back-row forwards, one used to debate whether, given an extended spell in the position, Paxton might develop into a Scottish counterpart to

Ireland's Donal Lenihan or John Beattie into a bethistled equivalent of South Africa's Frik du Preez. Even in the wet, Beattie contrived to look more like a potential du Preez against England at Murrayfield than Paxton had a Lenihan at Twickenham the previous March. He had been on the field less than a minute when he rose to an English drop-out at the start of the second half and deflected it down to Calder.

Moving blind behind a Calder swiftly buttressed by brother forwards, Laidlaw hoisted a teasing punt which confounded both Hare and Mike Slemen. The omnipresent Calder ripped the ball from clawing English hands and gave to Alan Tomes. Endowed with so many enviable attributes, the Hawick lock has perhaps not always played to his potential down the years but he won back his place to play a significant and often under-estimated part in this 1984 campaign. And now as he drove into the ruck, Leslie was at his shoulder, clearing a passage with the tigerish commitment of his own drive.

There is a world of difference from possession that is static or, worse, heaped back upon the halves from forwards in retreat and possession bequeathed by such a surge. With the English defence already badly shredded, Laidlaw served Rutherford. The stand-off picked up the pass on the bounce and Euan Kennedy, with Clive Woodward having been tempted in on to Rutherford in a vain attempt to stifle man and ball, called for the pass and swept in at just the right angle to burst clean through a yawning hole he had quick-wittedly anticipated would materialize. It gave both tries to Watsonians while the dexterity with which Rutherford (who, curiously enough, had once been on the Watson's staff) gathered and gave bore the touch of a craftsman.

The conversion by Dods gave Scotland a 12–3 lead. Almost at once, as Scotland were penalized for elbowing, Hare kicked what was his second penalty from six attempts. But the only further scoring was to be two more penalty goals from Dods. John Hall of Bath had just come on for the injured Peter Winterbottom when Robertson fielded superbly on the right touchline from Hare and John Scott was penalized for obstructing Kennedy amid the aftermath of Robertson's high infield punt for the first of the Gala full-back's penalty goals. Jim Pollock was on for Kennedy, who had damaged ligaments below the right knee, with Robertson moving into the centre, when, in the dying minutes, John Carleton and Huw Davies saved at the feet of a hack-and-chase rush spearheaded by Rutherford and were adjudged to have lain illegally over the ball. Dods again kicked the goal.

Above Scotland tackled magnificently. An Alan Tomes tackle about to disrupt, impolitely, a cosy transfer from Nick Youngs to his captain, Peter Wheeler. *Dave Stranock*

Below The covering John Carleton is left a thwarted bystander as Euan Kennedy dives triumphantly over the England line for Scotland's second try, thereby completing a famous Watsonian double. *Bob Thomas*

Thus, in treacherous goal-kicking conditions, ten of Scotland's points had come from Dods, who had converted both tries and been successful with two of his four penalty attempts, whereas Hare, over the match, had kicked only two penalty goals out of eight. For the first time in all the years she had watched him, Hare's wife had slipped quietly from the ground, unable to bear the sight any longer, interpreting the remaining play only from the volume of cheering.

Hare's goal-kicking had but compounded a sorry afternoon for the man whose normally trusty right boot had so often come to his country's rescue. Nor had he been helped by the fact that Rutherford had at once detected that both Carleton and Slemen were lying almost unbelievably flat in conditions which suggested that Scotland were much more likely to kick than run. Remembering the description by the late Carwyn James of that fateful afternoon in Dunedin, one was not surprised to find Chris Rea, the quicksilver little Scotland and Lions centre three-quarter who had been an eyewitness, likening Rutherford's tormenting of Hare to the demolition job Barry John had done on Fergie McCormick thirteen years previously.

In winning the hundredth encounter – as they had won the first – Scotland won the Calcutta Cup for the thirty-fourth time to the forty-four wins of England. Aitken became only the fourth Scot to captain his country to consecutive Calcutta Cup wins, his predecessors being J. D. Boswell (in 1893 and 1894), Dan Drysdale (1926 and 1927) and Peter Brown (1971 and 1972).

Deans, who had shared the tight-heads at 1–1 with Wheeler, had done nothing to alter one's opinion that Scotland have never had a more consistent forward nor, pound for pound, a better one. He was still carrying an injury from the Welsh match which handicapped him mainly when getting length on his throw-in and, anyway, since it was a less than perfect day for that particular tactic, Leslie was perhaps always going to be a less prolific source of tail of the line-out ball than he had been against Wales, even without the improved calibre of the immediate opposition. Yet the back row were again a veritable host in themselves.

Jim Aitken had sworn after the Welsh match that Scotland would keep their feet on the ground and that there would be no talk of a Triple Crown until England had been beaten. Even now, the Scottish top brass in the persons of Ian MacGregor, Jim Telfer and Jim Aitken were at pains to make sure that no one got carried away. It was an aim in which, paradoxically, they were assisted by the worries created by the tendency of the Scotland players to

As David Leslie competes for this throw-in with England's John Scott, Jim Calder comes round in the sweeping, supporting role in which he excels – so much so that England themselves had recourse to such a sweeper in their back row before the season was out. *Bob Thomas*

surrender another ten metres at penalties for what the referee, David Burnett, clearly took to be verbal dissent rather than polite enquiries as to the precise nature of the offence.

Ian MacGregor deemed it 'maybe understandable but still inexcusable' and, though Dusty Hare was now behind them, Ollie Campbell or Tony Ward lurked hard ahead. As was remarked, to invite such goal-kickers to move ten metres nearer your own posts is as foolhardy as offering Jack Nicklaus the use of the ladies' tees.

'A thrashing,' had been the rueful verdict at no-side of Peter Robbins, that legendary England flanker of yesteryear, and there was general agreement that Scotland had actually played better than in winning at Cardiff. Of course, they had been at home but then this was the first victory at Murrayfield since the building of the new East stand.

Aside from the fear that the cost would keep away many of rugby's more regular followers and countless youngsters – Jimmy Ireland, hooker in the 1925 Grand Slam side, had suggested many moons ago that the right compromise was to build a cover for the terracing but otherwise leave it alone – the suspicion had begun to gain ground that Murrayfield without the East terracing was like Anfield without the Kop or Sydney without the Hill.

Victory on that score was all the more welcome as the new stands at the Arms Park had seemed to render the normally magnificent and moving singing of the Welsh oddly muted and discordant. So much so as to prompt on the night of the match much apposite recounting of that yarn that the BBC's Alun Williams used to relate of the Welsh team on tour in New Zealand singing the songs of home and one elderly gentleman in the corner showing increasingly tearful signs of distress.

'You must be a Welshman?' had come the kindly and compassionate question.

'No,' he had replied, sorrowfully, 'a musician.'

THE ENGLISH VIEW
David Irvine with Dick Greenwood

At the time it was as though a great weight had been lifted from England's shoulders. At the time it scarcely seemed to matter that the All Blacks side which lost at Twickenham on 19 November 1983 was probably the weakest ever to leave New Zealand's shores. At the time England's victory by 15–9 was being seen in psychological terms, if no other, as the dawning of a new era. At the time.

Few seemed to care or notice that another eleven weeks – almost a third of the season – would pass before England returned to the international arena again. And for their hundredth meeting, no less, with the auld enemy, Scotland. Not, one must stress, that anyone close to the England camp was rash enough to risk a public assumption that the Five Nations Championship was within their grasp. Yet it was possible to detect an unaccustomed air of confidence.

It was the England coach, that hard-headed Lancastrian Dick Greenwood, who struck a cautionary note in a New Year's Eve interview when he warned that the New Zealand triumph could prove as easily a cul-de-sac as a cornerstone. 'There's always a danger of complacency in amateur sport,' he said. 'We smile smugly and think: haven't we done well? But the real answer is that it is what happens next that counts.'

And what happened next was that, though England were able to travel to Murrayfield with fourteen of the side that beat the All Blacks – Huw Davies replacing the injured Paul Dodge at centre – they still lost 18–6. As Greenwood had secretly feared, the long wait had been too long. The momentum had gone. The New Zealand performance had become irrelevant.

'There was nothing wrong with our thinking or planning,' he said. 'The players were simply inadequate.' Against New Zealand, and for a variety of reasons, they had played emotionally, technically and tactically far beyond themselves. 'But when it came to Scotland it was the Scots who performed our battle-plan far better than we could have hoped to.'

Did that suggest, then, that England had lacked the necessary motivation second time out? 'I think it must be accepted that our attitude was very different against the All Blacks. Five of the side wanted to prove a point because they hadn't been picked for the Lions' summer tour; five had been to New Zealand, were stuffed, and felt that they too had something to prove; and the other five simply got carried along. One's natural assumption was that they could produce a similar quality performance a second time. They didn't.'

Not that he thought that in any way detracted from Scotland's performance. Not only did Greenwood acknowledge their tactical superiority but he admitted that their level of commitment totally outshone England's. 'We didn't even register on the scale. That was perhaps the greatest disappointment.'

Scotland's ability to fling their opponents to the ground behind almost every ruck and maul, he felt, was of crucial importance; though he did question the legality of it. 'There again, what's legal? If it's not penalized, then it's legal on the day – therefore their tactical appreciation was absolutely 100 per cent correct.'

But was he suggesting the Irish referee, David Burnett, had favoured Scotland? 'Put it this way. David Leslie played the off-side laws to the limit. But let's not be naïve. That's one of the departments of good back-row forward play, assessing what is "on" on the day and taking maximum advantage of what is allowed.'

Of all the Scots, he thought, no one had made a greater contribution than the stand-off John Rutherford. 'How can you argue with a 100 per cent record? One pass in the entire game and it leads to a try. His judgement was perfect, he couldn't be faulted in any way. And Roy Laidlaw's support was crucial too and, when either one kicked, they chose the right club and hit the green every time.'

Unlike the England half-backs, who were under far greater pressure, the Scots were given a working platform thanks to what Greenwood called 'the magnificent self-effacing but destructive' back-row play of Leslie, Jim Calder and Iain Paxton allied to the reliable and robust work of the front five.

'The whole adrenalin factor, the whole emotional side of it, was seen in Roger Baird's performance on the left wing.

Baird chased about five times as hard as he probably has in his life. He did nothing with the ball in his hands – he wasn't given it – but he discomfited John Carleton and Dusty Hare repeatedly by arriving far quicker than anyone anticipated.'

One factor, felt Greenwood, over which they had no control was the weather. That transformed the match in Scotland's favour. 'Once the rain came I think it was very much a decision made on the day to play as they did and the whole beauty of Scotland's battle-plan was that it required no decisions to be made on the field.' England, on the other hand, needed to adapt and failed to do so.

The key moment came with Scotland's opening try by David Johnston, a score which Greenwood believed should have been prevented. 'I don't know whether it should be regarded as Scottish opportunism or downright fortuitous nonsense on the part of the England centres. How do you fault someone who doesn't have the technique to make a straightforward fly-hack? The idiot missed the bloody ball!

'What most annoyed me was that we had worked extremely hard on their imaginative use of the long throw used so effectively against Wales. That one simply flew into space and should have been hoofed to the half-way line.'

Would the course of the game have been altered had that ball been cleared? 'A general orgy of ifs and buts is pointless. If Dusty Hare had kicked a few, if we had made that fly-hack, if this, if that . . . it didn't happen. It was Scotland's year. They created their luck and every side needs luck to be successful.'

Greenwood did not feel, however, that Scotland's contribution to the game in the broadest sense was significant. 'But they eventually learned some sense, didn't they? For years they won no ball and were brilliant counter-attackers. Then they had a spell of winning the ball and not having a clue what to do with it. This time they decided that if they didn't think too hard and simply kicked, what ball they won could be useful. Is that not therefore the most efficient way to set about winning a Grand Slam?'

4

For Crown and Country

IRELAND (9) v SCOTLAND (32)

Played at Lansdowne Road, Dublin, 3 March 1984

IRELAND		SCOTLAND
15 J. J. Murphy (Greystones)	*Full-back*	15 P. W. Dods (Gala)
14 T. M. Ringland (Ballymena)	*Right wing*	14 J. A. Pollock (Gosforth)
13 M. J. Kiernan (Lansdowne)	*Centre*	13 K. W. Robertson (Melrose)
12 M. C. Finn (Cork Constitution)	*Centre*	12 D. I. Johnston (Watsonians)
11 K. D. Crossan (Instonians)	*Left wing*	11 G. R. T. Baird (Kelso)
10 A. J. P. Ward (St Mary's College)	*Stand-off*	10 J. Y. Rutherford (Selkirk)
9 J. A. P. Doyle (Greystones)	*Scrum-half*	9 R. J. Laidlaw (Jedforest)
1 P. A. Orr (Old Wesley)	*Loose-head prop*	1 J. Aitken (**captain**) (Gala)
2 H. T. Harbison (Bective Rangers)	*Hooker*	2 C. T. Deans (Hawick)
3 D. C. Fitzgerald (Lansdowne)	*Tight-head prop*	3 I. G. Milne (Heriot's FP)
4 M. I. Keane (Lansdowne)	*Lock*	4 A. J. Campbell (Hawick)
5 D. G. Lenihan (Cork Constitution)	*Lock*	5 A. J. Tomes (Hawick)
6 J. B. O'Driscoll (London Irish)	*Flanker*	6 J. H. Calder (Stewart's Melville FP)
7 D. G. McGrath (UCD)	*Flanker*	7 D. G. Leslie (Gala)
8 W. P. Duggan (**captain**) (Blackrock College)	*No. 8*	8 I. A. M. Paxton (Selkirk)

REPLACEMENTS
16 G. A. J. McLoughlin (Shannon)
17 J. L. Cantrell (Blackrock College)
18 D. E. Spring (Bagneres)
19 R. J. M. McGrath (Wanderers)
20 H. C. Condon (London Irish)
21 H. P. MacNeill (Oxford University and
    Blackrock College)

REPLACEMENTS
16 N. A. Rowan (Boroughmuir)
17 R. Cunningham (Bath)
18 J. R. Beattie (Glasgow Acads)
19 I. G. Hunter (Selkirk)
20 D. S. Wyllie (Stewart's Melville FP)
21 A. R. Irvine (Heriot's FP)

Referee F. A. Howard; touch judges J. A. F. Trigg and R. C. Quittenton
(Rugby Football Union)

When the no-alcohol ban was imposed at Murrayfield one mischievous rascal had enquired if the coach carrying the officials would enjoy diplomatic immunity. Many among the Scottish Rugby Union, mark you, must have come perilously close to taking not to their bus but to the wagon when George Crerar, for whose passing they had observed a minute's silence at a function the previous evening, blithely materialized at the Calcutta Cup.

'How could they tell?' asked a puzzled Dorothy Parker when they told her president Calvin Coolidge was dead and, to be honest, one could not but think of one or two SRU dignitaries over the years whose demise might have elicited a not dissimilar reaction. But Crerar, SRU president in 1969–70, would not have been among them and his disconcerting resurrection turned out to have been simply a case of mistaken identity.

Raising the dead happened to be just about the one power with which Jim Aitken had not been credited as the nation stood back in awe of a record, since taking over as Scotland's captain, of away wins at Twickenham and Cardiff, a home draw with the All Blacks and the retention at Murrayfield of the Calcutta Cup.

Aitken himself had kept it all very much in perspective. Over a beer at Murrayfield after a mid-week Scotland squad session, he had shown himself likeably aware of all the various factors which go towards the making of a winning or losing captain, which have little to do with him personally in that they are outside his control. Nor had he lost sight of the fact that he had been captain of the Blues, or Scotland XV, when they lost 21–3 to the Whites in the national trial, which had been jocularly but accurately predicted as Scotland's only defeat of the winter campaign.

Nothing he did all season with regard to the captaincy – and he did much – was more important than the ice-cold reality with which he kept dousing his troops. 'If we don't beat Ireland,' he said, that night at Murrayfield, 'we will have done nothing.' Not wholly true but it made sense to banish negative apprehension with a positive approach in which, as David Coleman would have said, they still had it all to do.

It was the sixth time since their last Triple Crown in 1938 that Scotland had arrived at the third match still in pursuit of that mythical but coveted crown, the last occasion being 1975 at Twickenham, from which agonizingly near miss only David Leslie survived within the Scottish ranks.

Much, in terms of omens, was made of the fact that Scotland won the last time they played a Triple Crown match in Ireland, in 1933 when the match was postponed till 1 April because of a brutal storm which had kept the ship bearing the Scottish team standing off Dublin Bay for sixteen hours. Incidentally, the assumption that if the scoring values had been the same as today Ireland, with their two tries to Scotland's two dropped goals, would have triumphed 8–6 instead of losing by that margin failed to take into account the different patterns of play according to whether you are in the lead or otherwise.

The build-up to the 1984 confrontation was delightfully Irish, with much talk of how many of that nation would actually like to see Scotland – traditionally bound to Ireland by the ancient quip that 'neither ever minded who beat the English' – rewarded with a Triple Crown. However, as Willie John McBride, the Ireland coach, noted pertinently, 'None among them happens to be in the Irish XV!'

The label of Dad's Army had become inextricably affixed to the Irish pack and one liked very much the laconic aside of Willie John that at least one of the advantages was that they were entitled to free travel. Their supporting press were a little taken aback to discover on arrival at Twickenham for the England match that the enemy actually averaged out at a year the older, though one Hibernian scribe, forced to retain geriatric among his sheathed adjectives, soon brightened at a thought which struck him. 'I wonder,' he said, shamelessly, 'if we might not have a go at them for sending such a young and inexperienced team to RFU headquarters.'

Scotland had two changes from the side which, a month previously, had come out at Murrayfield to defeat England. Euan Kennedy, whose damaged ligaments below the right knee had necessitated his leg being put in plaster, had, of course, not recovered. Nor had Bill Cuthbertson, the groin injury he suffered in the Calcutta Cup having played up after he returned for his club, Harlequins, in their John Player Cup tie with Plymouth Albion. Keith Robertson therefore continued in the centre, where he had finished the match against England, with Jim Pollock on the right wing. Pollock's reputation as a lucky mascot had become so firmly entrenched that there was even an impish suggestion that, when he was not in the side, he should be allowed to dress up in Scotland togs and lead the team out in the manner of the small boys in league football.

One had been aghast at the proposal that Tom Smith, who had done well in both his international appearances and been unlucky that injury had contributed to the loss of his place, should be brought in to partner Tomes. There would have been a definite case for that combination against, say, Rumania in Bucharest, to combat the lofty line-out expertise of the men from the land of Dracula, but it would have been altogether too stately a pairing to field against the Irish who, from time immemorial, have loved nothing better than getting in among an enemy line-out bordering on the statuesque. Mercifully, the Scottish selectors had not forgotten what happened when Smith and Tomes were partners against the All Blacks for the South at Netherdale and they rightly saw Smith as the alternative to Tomes but Alister Campbell as the alternative to Cuthbertson. In other words, they adhered roughly to that blend of workhorse and main jumper which has made for the most successful couplings at lock since the era of Marques and Currie and no doubt many another partnership back in the mists of antiquity.

The 25-year-old Campbell boasts the improbable nickname for such a husk of Hawick of Sally but not since Gracie Fields' heyday had it been roared so affectionately from so many lips as it was that afternoon at Lansdowne Road. He was the first of the season's conquering B team, who had beaten Ireland 21–3 at the Greenyards and France 13–10 in Albi, to graduate to a full cap, though he was to be joined in that honour in mid-match by Gordon Hunter.

Ireland, with Tony Ward continuing at stand-off in the enforced absence of Ollie Campbell, had made two alterations to the side which lost to England. John Murphy, once on the books of Arsenal and capped in South Africa two years previously and again in 1982 when he came on as the replacement for the injured David Irwin against Wales, displaced Hugo MacNeill, the British Lions full-back. At flank forward, the 22-year-old, 6ft-3in Derek McGrath, who had gone down with the ship when Ireland B were riddled by their Scottish counterparts in Melrose but who had previously been hailed as the 'new Slattery', came in for Willie Duncan. Ciaran Fitzgerald, the 1983 Lions captain, whose presence had kept Deans out of the Test team, was not selected for the match, and though nominated as a replacement, eventually withdrew through injury.

On the eve of the match in the team's headquarters at Kilternan, in the Dublin foothills, Jim Telfer wound up a session of studying previous matches on video-tape by saying, deceptively casually, that he personally was going for dinner but there was ten minutes more film he would like them to watch. He then left the room and ten of the eleven Borderers in the Scotland XV for the morrow found themselves sitting and squirming through the later stages of the South's rout at the hands of Stu Wilson's All Blacks at Netherdale. It was a period in which the All Blacks were, as Rutherford, shuddering in recollection, put it, 'running through us at will.' Any last delusions of grandeur cultivated in the three previous internationals were never going to survive that.

Bernard Darwin, the great golf writer, used to say that every match had a turning point and, if that is true of rugby, it was on this occasion arguably before a ball had been kicked – namely, when Willie Duggan, the Irish captain, won the toss and chose to play into the strong wind in the hope that it would be at least twenty minutes before a Scotland XV with so much at stake settled. Aitken would certainly have played with the wind had he won the toss, particularly in view of Ireland's Triple Crown match two years before when Scotland chose to play against the wind and then found it veering, producing from Jim Telfer the dry comment that it was 'A game of two halves, and Ireland had them both.'

In four minutes, Scotland were four points ahead. Paxton deflected the throw from Deans down to Campbell who peeled round the tail and set up the ruck perfectly, Laidlaw flashing right on the now widened blind side and jinking brilliantly inside four covering Irishmen for a truly memorable try. The late John Bannerman, who had so hated to see Scottish forwards merely serving their backs slavishly, would have relished the preliminary forward thrust which had dented the defence ball in hand much as his generation were wont to do with an attacking wheel and dribble.

Dods kicked the goal and four minutes later the Irish front row, which had been in similar trouble at Twickenham, were penalized for collapsing a scrum almost underneath their own posts and Dods clipped over the penalty goal. Shortly, Duggan was penalized for going over the ball in the on-the-ground grovelling at the back of the line-out and again Dods accepted the simple offering.

With twenty-five minutes gone, Scotland, changing to pack 3-3-2 close to the Irish line and wheeling against an Irish pack which had shown at Twickenham that it could be spun, were threatening a score by Paxton or, more likely, Leslie when Duggan, who had broken off, dived in at their feet. The referee, Fred Howard, a debutant in the international arena as Owen Doyle had been in Cardiff, unhesitatingly awarded the penalty try.

Dods duly slotted the straightforward conversion and a mere five minutes later, Laidlaw, in what could momentarily have been mistaken for an action replay of his try against Ireland in 1983, fed the scrum and, aided by the way it wheeled against the tight-head, shot blind to slice through an Irish defence again left somewhat flat-footed. Both of Laidlaw's tries had been scored within yards of each other and Laidlaw's Corner, as Chris Rea suggested so aptly in the *Scotsman*, was surely destined to take its place in the lore of Scottish rugby.

Since the coming of the hindmost foot off-side law, the angle of break in his second try was difficult to police against a player of Laidlaw's dart and quickness of foot, just as many a sevens stand-off has scored by speeding blind on a diagonal slant, the tackle so often going in just as the player crashes over the line.

Laidlaw took a bang on the head. At half-time, he was replaced by Gordon Hunter who had understudied to him on the tours of New Zealand in 1981 and Australia in 1982 and who had fifteen times been an international replacement, always to the Jedforest scrum-half. Even in these days of squad sessions, when the players practise together so much, it was still a bonus that Hunter was Rutherford's club partner. Early in the second half, Hunter was penalized for spoiling prematurely round the scrum and John Murphy, who had earlier missed a relative sitter, this time kicked the goal.

The Irish forwards were now doing much better in all phases and even the dynamism of the Scottish driving and rucking had notably subsided. Before the match, Jim Telfer had warned his players that Mr Howard was liable to be very strict in the second phase. Afterwards, Telfer felt that, with so much of the second-half game into the wind and therefore played within range of the Scottish posts, his players had quite often been prepared to lose a second-phase ball rather than risk a penalty. There was also, though, the inescapable fact that, with Ireland learning from Scotland's tactics in the first half and using the wind so effectively in much of their own kicking, the ratio of attacking and defensive rucks naturally changed sides.

More than a quarter of the match still remained when Ireland scored again. The eager Hunter was off-side at a scrum but the

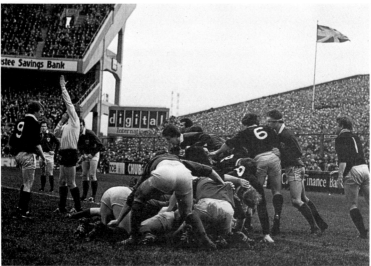

Above The scuttling speed on the break, which brought Laidlaw two great tries at Lansdowne Road, graphically depicted beneath the spreading wingspan of Alan Tomes. *George Herringshaw*

Below The penalty try for Scotland in which the referee, Fred Howard, ruled that the Irish captain, Willie Duggan, had plunged illegally into Scotland's scrum but for which 'a try would probably have been scored'.
George Herringshaw

referee played advantage. After Willie Duggan had picked up and exchanged passes with Tony Doyle before combining with McGrath, Moss Finn worked a dummy scissors with Michael Kiernan for Kiernan to shear through the Scottish midfield for what was Ireland's only try of the championship.

Murphy converted but, in the fading minutes of an historic match, Scotland cut loose. Like every other team, they had code names for their various moves which, with Jim Telfer's tenure of office at an end, are no longer classified information. Just as the ploy which brought Paxton's try from a free-kick at Cardiff answered to 'Grand Stand', so the call of 'France' meant that Johnston was about to come back from centre to blaze on to the scrum-half's pass going blind in a gambit the Scots picked up from Codorniou, the French centre. It all but brought that long-awaited first try for Baird, the only one of the present Scotland backs never to have had his name on the score-sheet, but Johnston had judged him to be covered and was himself hit hard in the tackle by Trevor Ringland.

Soon, though, Campbell turned the ball back from the throw-in and Hunter swung wide round the back of the line-out before giving to Rutherford. He jinked inside Finn to cut through and send in Robertson for a splendidly taken try which Dods comfortably converted.

The next try was, in its own way, a toast to Absent Friends, for it was code-named 'Jimbo' after Jim Renwick who had employed it to such effect with Hawick. He had been for so long at the heart and soul of this Scotland team only to miss out on this season of seasons. Paxton picked up at a set scrum and passed back to Rutherford who came left with Robertson, coming from right of the scrum, to appear in the line outside the stand-off for the ball to go out through Johnston to Baird who, accomplished footballer that he is, timed the scoring pass perfectly for Dods to go in at the corner. A great try any day and a masterly one with which to ring down the curtain on a Triple Crown, while one doubts if Herbert Waddell and the Oxford three-quarter line ever moved the ball more sweetly.

After the Second Test in New Zealand in 1981 when Scotland, without playing all that badly, lost by a try-score of 7–1, a New Zealand journalist had had the temerity to ask Telfer blandly if he knew if that was truly a record score. Telfer had replied bleakly that the New Zealander was the newspaper man and it was up to him to know these things. One could not help feeling that the wheel had rather nicely come full circle when an Irish writer asked

Above Now the most capped of all Scotsmen with fifty-two, Jim Renwick missed out on Scotland's Grand Slam year but his name was still stamped all over the move which brought Scotland's fifth and final try. *George Herringshaw*

Below Scotland's fourth try with Keith Robertson crossing the Irish line despite Trevor Ringland's last-ditch tackle. *Bob Thomas*

exactly the same thing at Lansdowne Road and got precisely the same answer.

A record it was, the highest score and the largest winning margin in the ninety-four matches between the two nations. The try score of 5–1 mirrored the try score in 1938 when, in Wilson Shaw's Match, the Triple Crown was last won. In Paris, the three Scotsmen over there as referee and touch judges for the France–England match were told the scoreline from Lansdowne Road and at first thought it a leg-pull.

The one unhappy note was that, with Laidlaw already doubtful for the French match because of his knock on the head, Hunter, in running from the field, had collided with a young spectator and collected a depressed fracture of the cheekbone, an injury very similar to the one he had sustained in New Zealand in 1981 and which was sure to rule him out of the game with France.

With sixteen points already to his name, Dods would have needed just that final conversion from the touch-line of his own try to break Andy Irvine's points record for a Scottish player in a championship match. Instead he had to be content with only equalling his illustrious predecessor's record. Fielding safely in that bothersome wind, Dods had again played soundly and well in a match in which Telfer's tactics had once more been unerringly pitched to the match in hand.

The tackling of the Irish centres against England, coupled with the team's limitations elsewhere, had argued that Ireland were likely to be at their most dangerous exploding loose ball in midfield. Unquestionably, they had the pace in Kiernan and Finn to exploit such shrapnel. Thus, it was rational for Scotland to attack, as they did, a good deal through their halves and back row while, bearing in mind the desirability of turning and stretching the Irish pack without giving Ireland much to knock over in midfield, the kicking of Laidlaw (until he was injured) and Rutherford was made to order.

All through Scotland had made their own breaks save that John Murphy had to take over the Irish goal-kicking and, eventually, Hugh Condon – from the substitutes bench – the stand-off berth, because Tony Ward had been sufficiently dazed to have trouble focusing. That was an affliction most of the Scottish supporters one met in the small hours of the night seemed to have found uncommonly catching.

Above Peter Dods at Lansdowne Road beneath a high ball, one of his greater strengths. *All-Sport*

Below The Scotland XV which won the Triple Crown and went on to win the Grand Slam. The players (left to right):
back row D. G. Leslie, L. G. Milne, I. A. M. Paxton, A. J. Tomes, A. J. Campbell, J. H. Calder, D. L. Johnston;
front row J. A. Pollock, K. W. Robertson, J. Y. Rutherford, J. Aitken (capt), R. J. Laidlaw, C. T. Deans, G. R. T. Baird, P. W. Dods. *Bob Thomas*

AS THE IRISH SAW IT
John Campbell with Willie John McBride

A combination of total commitment, the ability to win the crucial fifty-fifty ball on the ground and the elegant skills of their scrum-half combined to take Scotland to their epic Triple Crown and Grand Slam triumphs last season.

That's the view of Willie John McBride for whom Scotland's Triple Crown clincher at Lansdowne Road in March signalled the end of a brief reign as Irish coach.

But McBride, ever a realist, is reluctant to dwell on the past: rather, he prefers to ponder the future and, in this respect, harbours no doubts that Scotland could remain a potent force for the next few seasons.

Firm foundations have obviously been laid and, according to McBride, the ingredients were encapsulated in that Lansdowne Road victory.

'There can be no doubt about it – Scotland were much superior on the day and thoroughly deserved to win,' asserted McBride. 'They revealed great heart and the basis for their success was laid at half-back and in their back row.'

McBride was quick to admit that Ireland played into Scotland's hands by electing to play against the strong wind in the opening half.

'This was, of course, a stupid decision,' stated McBride. 'Let's be honest, we gave the Scots a helping hand by doing this – and they certainly made the most of it.'

If the Scottish triumph was fashioned by their efficient, mobile pack it was the work of executioner-in-chief Roy Laidlaw that really broke Irish hearts. He provided the flair, panache and, most important of all, the scoring touch that effectively underlined the main differences between the sides – not just on the day but throughout the Five Nations campaign.

'Yes, Laidlaw was a real thorn in our side. I honestly believed that we had devised tactics to contain him but when the match got going there was simply no way he was to be stopped,' confessed McBride. 'I must say that I was extremely disappointed that we were unable to shackle him. Had we succeeded in this respect, then I am convinced that the eventual outcome might well have been a lot different.'

The initial nails in Ireland's coffin were hammered in when Laidlaw darted in for his brace of first-half tries and the lid was put fimly in place when the Scottish back row of Jim Calder, Iain Paxton and David Leslie completely snuffed out the Irish bid to claw their way back into the match.

'The Scottish strategy was tailor-made for the occasion,' reminisced McBride. 'Laidlaw refused to let the ball out until his side had opened up a gap on the scoreboard and then the pack took over to force us into submission. It was simple, yet

Roy Laidlaw (left) with the manager, Willie John McBride, on the Lions 1983 tour of New Zealand. By a twist of fate it was a brace of tries by Laidlaw at Lansdowne Road, which did much to bring the legendary Irishman's short reign as Ireland's coach to an end. *Bob Thomas*

totally effective and a sharp lesson in how to play to the best of your strengths.'

And while McBride admitted that he had been prepared for Scotland's all-action forward play revolving around their back row, he could only watch in a mixture of disbelief and grudging admiration as Laidlaw, one of the most consistent performers for the Lions under McBride's management in New Zealand some months earlier, proceeded to imprint his name indelibly upon the game.

Scotland's later tries were, in the opinion of McBride, products of their adventurous policy – a policy that had in the recent past backfired on them but which, ultimately, proved their passport to immortality. 'Indeed, throughout the championship, Scotland recorded scores of rare quality and there was certainly a lot of admiration for their bold approach and cavalier tactics at Lansdowne Road,' emphasized McBride.

While he was shell-shocked by the manner in which Ireland capitulated, McBride was quick to laud the efforts of Jim Telfer, with whom he had soldiered throughout a long, hard tour of New Zealand last summer and a coach for whom the big Ulsterman has the healthiest respect.

'Jim showed patience and commitment with the Scots for a couple of years before they finally hit it off. It was by no means an overnight success, just a reward for a lot of painstaking work and absolute dedication,' remarked McBride. 'Remember, Scotland had endured a very lean spell up until last season, never having managed to attain the consistency level to gain a Triple Crown or championship. But they went the full way last year and Jim Telfer deserves a large slice of credit for helping them achieve their goal.'

If the manner of Ireland's demise alarmed McBride, he certainly did not spend any time seeking excuses to condone his side's shortcomings: 'Often, a negative approach can be adopted in this respect by blaming the conditions or the referee but, while we did ourselves no favours by playing against the wind in the first half, there are no mitigating circumstances. On the day Scotland held all the aces and we were made to look a poor side.'

Grand Slam and Triple Crown accolades invariably evoke recourse to the word 'great' in relation to the sides involved.

But could the Scottish side that covered themselves in glory last season be termed a great team?

'Well, not quite,' mused McBride. 'They were a team who played to their maximum ability and showed a wonderful sense of purpose throughout the championship.'

He went on: 'The level of commitment was magnificent and I must say that I have rarely seen such fine work achieved by a back row in tandem with their half-backs. The team were a fine advertisement for rugby football. Perhaps if they continue to serve up this particular brand of play they will earn the label of a truly great side. After all, success generally breeds success.'

'Scotland,' concluded McBride, 'had to exercise patience in their wait for glory but failure beforehand obviously made their triumph all the more sweet. They'll be difficult to shift now.'

5

The Day

SCOTLAND (21) v FRANCE (12)
Played at Murrayfield, 17 March 1984

SCOTLAND		FRANCE
15 P. W. Dods (Gala)	Full-back	15 S. Blanco (Biarritz)
14 J. A. Pollock (Gosforth)	Right wing	14 J. Begu (Dax)
13 K. W. Robertson (Melrose)	Centre	13 P. Sella (Agen)
12 D. I. Johnston (Watsonians)	Centre	12 D. Codorniou (Narbonne)
11 G. R. T. Baird (Kelso)	Left wing	11 P. Esteve (Narbonne)
10 J. Y. Rutherford (Selkirk)	Stand-off	10 J-P. Lescarboura (Dax)
9 R. J. Laidlaw (Jedforest)	Scrum-half	9 J. Gallion (Toulon)
1 J. Aitken (captain) (Gala)	Loose-head prop	1 P. Dospital (Bayonne)
2 C. T. Deans (Hawick)	Hooker	2 P. Dintrans (Tarbes)
3 I. G. Milne (Heriot's FP)	Tight-head prop	3 D. Dubroca (Agen)
4 A. J. Campbell (Hawick)	Lock	4 F Haget (Biarritz)
5 A. J. Tomes (Hawick)	Lock	5 J Condom (Boucau)
6 J. H. Calder (Stewart's Melville FP)	Flanker	6 J-P. Rives (captain) (Racing Club de France)
7 D. G. Leslie (Gala)	Flanker	7 J-L. Joinel (Brive)
8 I. A. M. Paxton (Selkirk)	No. 8	8 J-C. Orso (Nice)

REPLACEMENTS
16 N. A. Rowan (Boroughmuir)
17 G. J. Callander (Kelso)
18 J. R. Beattie (Glasgow Acads)
19 S. G. Johnston (Watsonians)
20 D. S. Wyllie (Stewart's Melville FP)
21 A. R. Irvine (Heriot's FP)

REPLACEMENTS
16 B. Herrero (Nice)
17 M. Cremaschi (Lourdes)
18 P. Lacans (Beziers)
19 P. Berbizier (Lourdes)
20 L. Pardo (Monteferrand)
21 G. Laporte (Graulhet)

Referee W. Jones; touch judges A. Richards and C. Norling (Wales)

There had been many an echo on the return home from Dublin of that moment in the sixties when, on the Sunday after an international, a plane bearing Scottish supporters and miscellaneous club players rose into the buffeting wind en route for Edinburgh. The Aer Lingus pilot's voice had rung out over the plane's loudspeaker system. 'I'm afraid,' he declaimed, cheerfully, 'that this flight is going to be very like your weekend – bloody rough!'

In winning what was their nation's ninth Triple Crown and the first for forty-six years, Scotland had done it the hard way with two of the three matches away from home. As to the SRU President, Adam Robson, he had taken his place alongside such soothsayers as Merlin, the three witches from Macbeth and Doug Smith, for had he not prophesied that Scotland would win the Triple Crown just as Smith had raised similarly polite titters in 1971 by forecasting that the Lions would win the Test series 2–1 with one match drawn.

Bill McMurtrie, of the *Glasgow Herald*, the only Scottish scribe to cover all three of the tours which had played such an important part in the evolution of the Grand Slam team – to France in 1980, New Zealand in 1981 and Australia in 1982 – is wont to lace his coverage with a statistical wizardry worthy of cricket's Bill Frindall.

On the morning of the French match, McMurtrie revealed that only in 1923 and 1978 had two countries with maximum points previously met in the final match of the championship. In those past two summit meetings, England had beaten Scotland at Inverleith sixty-one years ago and Wales thwarted France.

Apart from the fact that even Scotland had to give best to France in the matter of those overseas tours – the Tricolors having been to South Africa in 1980, Australia in 1981, Argentina in 1982 and Australia again in 1983 – Jim Telfer, where others might have feared that it would end up with the French being shown just too much respect, hammered into the players that the enemy ahead were a very different proposition from their previous victims.

'We must measure ourselves against the best,' he said more than once, 'and that to me means, in a world context, a full strength New Zealand and, within our own International Championship, France.'

Telfer was not forgetting what has passed into the Welsh archives as that country's second Golden Era, the years of Barry John, Phil Bennett and company. But to him in modern times, 'It is the French who usually have the best players'.

Telfer stressed, 'You can never entirely deny them good ball, because of their quickness of technique and improvisation and when they suddenly catch fire they are liable to burn you as no other side. 'If it had been France and not Ireland who were on top in that spell in the second half,' Telfer opined, bluntly, 'they might have had eighteen points on the board before we knew quite what had hit us.'

The widely proclaimed weakness of France in 1984 had lain in their front five but taking the stuffing out of the Gallic tight quintet had been made a lot more difficult by the recall of Pierre Dospital to loose-head. There was, too, the need to contain Jean-Luc Joinel at the back of the line-out, especially as ball won from that vicinity was liable to be a lot more inviting for backs to run than even the beautiful two-handed catching of Donal Lenihan had been able to spawn from No. 2 at Lansdowne Road.

Scotland had mostly rucked superbly throughout the season and not least against the All Blacks themselves but, as with the Springboks, some of the best French second-phase ball can spring unrucked from the broken play. Which can ask different questions of the quickness of foot and speed of reaction of the opposition's defence . . .

Jean Piquet, the French counterpart to Colin Telfer in terms of coaching the outsides, had gone on record as saying that the French back division were the best ever to emanate from that extravagantly talented rugby nation. In particular, Jerome Gallion was back and not only as a vintage scrum-half who could be exceedingly dangerous in his own right but as the man to call the shots – a duty behind the scrum which had passed in the Scotland team from Rutherford as stand-off to Laidlaw, one of the advantages being the obviously greater ease of communication between Aitken and the scrum-half.

Not for nothing does Ireland's lightly-built Tony Doyle answer to 'Gandhi', but the quick and chunky Gallion was going to be another thing again. Gallion, admittedly, also frequently pivots in order to pass off the thrust of his left hand but the difference in the quickness and flexibility of his standing pass when so doing and Tony Doyle's as yet too often painfully telegraphed dive-pass at Lansdowne Road was sure to make it much more difficult for the Scottish breakaways to take aim.

Outside the French halves were lashings of pace and flair, with Didier Codorniou a class centre, Patrick Esteve blisteringly swift and, at full-back, one of the most lethal of latent threats in Serge Blanco, a richly endowed player always capable of running back at you with a vengeance anything in the way of a loose kick.

All winter the Scottish kicking had been shrewdly tailored to the game in hand. A Blanco in league with auxiliary full-backs of the speed and verve of Jacques Begu and Esteve suggested that the assorted diagonals by Rutherford which had served Scotland so well against England and Ireland would be used much more sparingly against France. Instead one would be looking for the kind of towering up-and-under off which even a Serge Blanco or an Andy Irvine is always going to find it much more difficult to run.

Telfer knew, too, that it is the French running off the ball, both fore and aft, and in those dangerous manoeuvres among back row and halves, which allow their handling skills full expression. That and the depth of their alignment behind the scrum.

There was a time in the post-war era when the deeper you lay, the farther behind the gain line you were apt to be hit. With the coming of the hindmost foot off-side law and, still more relevantly, the ten-yards-back restriction at the line-out – now ten metres – backs were compelled to lie by law where once they lay by convention. So far as was humanly possible within the contemporary laws, Scotland had pressurized their opponents all season but they took the field against France with the backs knowing that they might have an awful long way to run to get to their men. Around the periphery of scrum, ruck and line-out, they would still be harrying stiflingly but the defence farther out would have to be more circumspect.

'Three-quarters need to be encouraged to draw the defence across the advantage line,' Guy Boniface had preached, reflecting the French thinking. 'You want the defender to come at you on a line parallel to the touch-line.'

All of which was a reminder that the Scots would have to balance their anxiety to engage the French backs before they reached the gain line against the folly of selling themselves in a headlong attempt to take man and ball together, or virtually so.

The Scots were unchanged from Dublin while the feature of the ultimate French selection was the extent of the reshuffle when Dominique Erbani, the Agen back-row forward whose height at the rear of the line-out had been a considerable factor in France's championship bid, withdrew because of influenza.

Francis Haget, the thirty-four-year-old Biarritz second-row forward who had returned to the game after a two-year break, came in at lock. Jean-Charles Orso, who had come on as a replacement against England – 'We have found our Beaumont,' the French coach, Jacques Fouroux, had claimed – dropped back to No. 8 with Joinel moving to the flank. Three changes for one. Jim Aitken read Haget's inclusion as a sign that France would not be averse to taking Scotland on up front, particularly in the first quarter. 'We mustn't be obsessed with the Grand Slam,' Fouroux had commented to *L'Equipe*'s Henri Garcia. 'A third Grand Slam in seven years would be fine but for me the feat of the season was winning in Cardiff. For Scotland the Grand Slam is something that an entire people have been awaiting since 1925.

'Their aim, above all, will be to win, even by a single point in the last minute. Rugby is about winning. But in the particular situation of the present French team – a team that enjoys their rugby and are giving pleasure to so many people – our goal is to make this finale an apotheosis by aiming very high. Besides, we don't have a side for minimum-risk rugby, Rumanian or Irish style. The game plan is to play to the hilt.'

The clans had invaded Dublin by boat and plane for the Triple Crown and now Edinburgh swarmed with 15,000 French, though pride of place in terms of loyal enthusiasm unarguably went to a Scot, the 29-year-old Andy Stuart-Menteith, who had emigrated to Australia ten years previously but unblinkingly forked out £1200 to fly home for the Grand Slam match. 'It may be a once in a lifetime chance to see a Scottish Grand Slam,' he explained – and after a fifty-nine years' gap no one was in any hurry to contradict him.

It had taken Scotland four minutes to open the scoring in the Triple Crown match and within three minutes they had the scoreboard moving in the Grand Slam encounter as Dods kicked a penalty goal. France had infringed the mandatory one-metre spacing at the line-out and, as David Leslie drove from Scotland's free-kick machination, Orso was adjudged to have tackled him illegally high.

For much of the rest of the first half it was all France, though the claim by Fouroux that for most of that period it looked like a First Division side visiting a Second Division team did less than justice not just to the gallantry of the Scottish defence but to its quality and maturity.

Telfer had emphasised again and again that, for all the talent and legerdemain of the Tricolors, 'Even French tries can generally be traced back to a missed tackle. Well though we have tackled this season, we may very likely have to tackle even better against France. Above all, that first tackle has got to go in and go in hard and unanswerably.'

In the whole of that long and pounding siege, France, who had arrived at Murrayfield having scored eight tries in the championship to Scotland's nine, managed just one try. With Scotland defending a left-hand blind side at a set scrum on France's ball, Orso picked up and sent Gallion slanting between the last-ditch tackles of Paxton and Baird for what was the scrum-half's ninth try for his country.

Obviously, the move had much in common with the Welsh try at Cardiff when Eddie Butler picked up and gave to Mark Douglas who did the damage for Titley to score but, for students of the game, the interesting thing was that the Scottish defence this time was different and rather more conventional. It was Calder who engaged the first man, Orso, with his No. 8, Paxton, moving out for the second man, Gallion, whereas it had been vice versa in Cardiff. Still more to the point was that the try underlined how infernally difficult such a port-side blind side can be to defend on the enemy ball, though possibly the defence could have done themselves a heap of good by moving into the tackle with a little more momentum.

Lescarboura converted but though there was still at least a quarter of an hour to go in the first half, France still led by just 6–3 at half-time. On the receiving end as they had been, Scotland had still contrived to pressurise much of the French possession, muck them up, but by far the biggest factor had been the penalty and free-kick count – eight against France before there was even one against Scotland.

Whatever anybody thought of the individual interpretations, it surely said something for Mr Winston Jones, in his first international as Owen Doyle had been in Cardiff and Fred Howard in Dublin, that he did not give the token penalty or two into which many another referee might have been tempted to redress the growing imbalance.

Referees notoriously can be short of friends and Scotland had their own reasons for feeling aggrieved. All season their rucking had been their trump card but now they found it difficult to bring it to bear under a referee who, quite simply, believed that it was better to blow for a scrum before a transgression on the floor compelled him to blow for a penalty. The mind went back to that afternoon in January 1964 when Scotland, playing magnificently, drew 0–0 at Murrayfield with the Fifth All Blacks who, it has to be conceded, were barely allowed to ruck at all by the referee.

Yet in the same way as the intelligence, integrity and zest of the Scottish defence had not a little to do with the missed French chances in that first half, so it has to be acknowledged that for most of the match the shock and sophistication with which the French hit them in the tackle was such that the Scots had a devil of a job not just to make the initial dent but even to end up still taking the tackle on their own terms.

It was quite something to behold for this pack were the best Scotland had had with regard to making the ball available and maybe the best in that respect there has yet been in Britain. Moreover, they had been well warned by Jim Telfer about what to expect but, as the Scotland coach said, such ferocity of aggressive defence is so far removed from what the players habitually encounter in British domestic rugby, so much more physical, that even this deeply experienced Scottish side required time to adjust.

In the second half, Gallion collided with David Leslie as the committed Scotland flanker contested an enemy line-out throw over the top intended for the French scrum-half. Gallion was carried off on a stretcher and afterwards there were stories that Jean-Pierre Rives, the French captain, had feared that Gallion had swallowed his tongue and that others had thought he was dead, their own subsequent contribution suffering in consequence. But the fact remains that he had come to before the stretcher had passed from sight.

The criticism of the treatment on offer, which later appeared in a medical journal, read all the more strangely in that that aspect of the SRU's activities has long been widely praised – the medicine men, principally comprising Donald Macleod as honorary surgeon, David McLean as physiotherapist and Dr Clark Sharp, being at once greatly respected by the players and very popular with them.

Pierre Berbizier came on as Gallion's replacement and when John Rutherford was brought down and penalised for playing the ball in the tackle, Lescarboura, a classic toe-kicker in an age when the round-the-corner method has become so much more fashionable in place-kicking that the scouts of American grid-iron football scour Europe where soccer is so much stronger than in the States, kicked a grand goal.

Joinel fastened on to a pass from the driving Leslie but he was tackled and penalised amid the aftermath. Dods, who soon after half-time had missed two kickable penalties, was back on target with his second penalty goal.

Robertson, so often useful in the bits and pieces, fielded and launched Campbell who drove in quest of a ruck. At that ruck Rives was penalised for being on the wrong side, an award transferred from inside the Scottish half to just short of the French ten-metres line on account of the indignant indiscipline of Philippe

Dintrans. Dods gratefully accepted the penalty now much more obviously within his range.

From a line-out and the tidying of Daniel Dubroca, Lescarboura dropped a long and lovely goal. Twelve–nine to France but Scotland drew level when Deans found Robertson with a long throw over a reduced line-out. Rutherford was up inside the centre and Leslie inside the stand-off and, as the sortie was checked, Orso was penalised for going over the ball. Yet again the French indiscipline – this time their captain, Rives – cost France a further ten metres and again Dods made them pay, this time from shorter range.

'The turning point,' Jim Telfer was to assert at the post-match press conference, 'was at 12–12 when Blanco was caught under a high ball and we carried him for twenty-five yards. I've never seen that before, and we scored immediately after it.'

Moving right from a scrum, Rutherford kicked high back across field with Baird and Johnston in searing pursuit, the kind of hounding which had accompanied so much of Scotland's kicking throughout the championship. The ball broke to Codorniou who found touch close to the French line.

At which point a flash-back is relevant. At Cardiff, when the Welsh line-out lost control of their own throw and Jim Aitken scored, the Welsh were criticised for not throwing to the front so close to their own line if they were not going to throw right over the back to their outsides. By that token, in now aiming for Paxton toward the tail, Deans was giving every chance for an accident to happen if the Scots did not actually win the tempting tail-of-the-line-out ball they were seeking.

Calder, anticipating a ricochet, had perhaps, as he said with cheerful honesty on television, moved a little off-side. At any rate, as the ball came down to him off the aerial clash of Paxton and Joinel, he dropped over the line for the most momentous try he will ever score: 'Just my distance . . .'

If some thought the ball had come forward to him off Paxton, Mr Winston Jones was not among them and it is fundamental to the whole ethos of rugby that the referee is accepted as the sole judge of fact though none, heaven knows, would claim to be infallible. It was singularly appropriate that it should have been Calder who got the historic try for he symbolised so much of Jim Telfer's reign. The kind of player who, if it were soccer and Jim Telfer a manager, he would always have wanted to take with him rather as Brian Clough used to take John McGovern.

Ubiquitous rather than fast, Calder makes up in speed of thought what he may lack in speed of foot. Sound rather than spectacular,

Above Winston Jones, the referee, stamps the seal of legitimacy on Jim Calder's Grand Slam try at Murrayfield. *Bob Thomas*

Below Twinned in destiny. Jim Calder (left) the Scotland try-scorer, with his captain, Jim Aitken, amid the heady aftermath of victory. *Bob Thomas*

he doubled the line-out value of the galvanic Scottish tail-gunner, David Leslie, by his wide-awake sweeping while his supreme ability to make the ball available stood out in a Scottish pack to whom that skill had become as natural as breathing.

Dods converted and, in injury-time, went to his fifty, as the cricket writers say, that total for the season being reached with a comparatively easy penalty goal awarded for Blanco's late tackle on Dods himself.

Because of the linguistic pitfalls, there was more than one version of what the French captain actually said at the post-match banquet. In essence, it was that while he, Jean-Pierre Rives, was often accused of thinking he was the referee, here was a referee who thought he was a player. What that meant was also open to interpretation but Mr Jones would have been hard put to take it exactly as a compliment and never mind the more conventional utterances which followed.

The French papers had no truck with such ambiguity: 'In all my years of trundling from one press box to the next,' declared Henri Nayrou in *Midi Olympique*, 'never have I seen such helplessness vis-a-vis a referee. One quickly sensed a deep malaise – five penalties against France in the first four minutes . . . The rapidity of some of the penalty calls brought to mind the Arab proverb, "Beat your wife every morning, and if you don't know why, she does." Frenchmen are not saints. Indeed they are regarded – and it's the absolute truth – as being the least disciplined lot on the international circuit. But here the gross disproportion in the punishment was a scandal.'

'If the British don't want us to win this Grand Slam,' Bob Donahue quoted Jean-Pierre Rives as writing in *L'Equipe*, 'there's a simple solution: we quit after the third match. I hope that remark will be translated and read in Britain. I don't feel I have lessons in courtesy – in fair play, as they call it – to receive from anyone across the Channel.'

Rives, though, had not lost his sense of humour, murmuring that France had still won the Triple Crown – a neat reference to the fact that they had, like Scotland, come into the Grand Slam match having already beaten Ireland, Wales and England. Nor a natural generosity.

'The Scots are a fine team,' he said. 'In their three matches against the other Home Unions they didn't have the help of the referee. They earned their Triple Crown and they are worthy of the Grand Slam. It's hard to win one, you know. So they are to be congratulated. I regret, we all regret, all thirty players (the Scots less than us, perhaps) that the real match didn't take place. The Scots might have had the wherewithal to beat us . . .'

The noted French rugby writer, Denis Lalanne, writing on the night after the match for *L'Equipe*, struck similar notes: 'Jean-Pierre Rives's team played a fabulous first half – to my mind, the greatest rugby display of pace and character ever achieved by a French side. The match left an aftertaste of disgust that may not soon be dispelled; at the least, a malaise has settled upon Franco-British relations. And yet this Scottish Grand Slam is frankly a pleasure. For it is safe to assume that many a Scottish side have deserved the Grand Slam since 1925 and especially in the past few years.'

In his report to the French Rugby Federation's annual congress, the President, Albert Ferrasse, rose above the result: 'During the past year, thanks to the new methods of communication we have developed, rugby's audience has increased considerably. According to the statisticians, rugby in France, with its 200,000 registered players and officials, has acquired an audience in France equivalent to that of tennis (one million registrations) and half that of soccer (two million registrations). Even if they didn't achieve the Grand Slam, the French team gave our game a good image. Soccer has Platini, we have Fouroux.'

All, of course, was very different in the Scottish camp. The focal figure for the congratulations was Jim Telfer. 'If anyone owes anything to anyone, it is the players who owe it to you, Jim,' quoth the captain, Jim Aitken. Ian MacGregor, convener of the Scottish selectors and himself the recipient of many a warm handshake, had a certain rhythm to his summation: 'Jim Telfer had the wish to do it, the will to do it, the chance to do it and the team to do it.'

The smile which had suffused Jim Telfer's honest and craggy countenance at Lansdowne Road had been positively seraphic and now he more than once broke into a broad grin. But mostly the smile which played about his lips had about it the satisfaction of a difficult job well done: 'You have to have good players, the commitment and the format – and, in our case, those ingredients had been fused over several seasons and three overseas tours.'

Scotland had sowed many of the seeds of victory with the type of dedicated scrummaging which eats farther into the entrails of the enemy the longer the game lasts. Good scrummaging is very much a collective effort but the contribution of Iain Milne against France had been such as, entirely justifiably, to entice Jim Telfer away from his normal practice of not singling out individuals.

If the Lions had had to play a Test match hard on top of the Five Nations Championship, Milne would have been my own unhesitating choice on the tight-head. Particularly as the scrums were breaking up, he took such stick in that French match as would have had many a highly paid British heavyweight boxing prospect writhing on the canvas. In scrummaging away regardless, he earned the undiluted, wondering admiration of colleagues never themselves in any danger of being accused of being either chicken or squeamish.

In these days of the eight-man shove, there are clear advantages in having a hooker of the size and bulk of Gary Callander who, in the absence of Colin Deans, won golden opinions in winning his first cap versus Rumania. But Deans has made light of his own comparative lack of weight and, without ever shirking the tighter chores, has shown throughout his career a speed about the field which rekindled a remark first made about Ireland's Ken Kennedy – that he was in danger of being had up before the Front Row Union for indecent exposure. Were all this not enough, the throwing in of the Hawick hooker, born of much assiduous practice, makes him in his own way as valuable at a line-out as any leaping specialist jumper.

Alongside his clubmate, Alan Tomes, the industrious and soundly schooled Campbell was an eloquent tribute to the driving coaching of Derrick Grant in Campbell's formative years. Paxton, always a gifted player in relation to build, pace and ball sense, had become much more assertive under the influence of Bill Dickinson's coaching at Selkirk and Jim Telfer's at international level and the Lions Test No. 8 could look back on a notably profitable championship.

As for David Leslie, he deservedly won *Rugby World*'s European Player of the Year award and his form his omission from the 1983 Lions tour. Maybe there were some grounds for the allegations which, assuredly, cost him that tour, that he was not a 'wide' player in the manner of a Graham Mourie – but, long before no-side and the climactic match of the Grand Slam, he would have been entitled to retort 'So what?'

Looking equally discredited long before the end of the championship were those suggestions earlier in the season that Roy Laidlaw's day was done, at least at international level. He is a different player with John Rutherford than he is with anyone else while his service has predictably improved greatly since he sought to achieve his effects by speed and accuracy rather than a length of pass he simply does not own.

Above Alan Tomes and Iain Paxton airborne versus Jean-Luc Joinel.
Colorsport

Below David Leslie driving. *Colorsport*

Besides, his ability to break in itself helps to give his stand-off room by taking some of the weight off him while Laidlaw, whose cover defence was among his most valuable attributes, is a born competitor who long ago learned to live on his wits behind a Jedforest pack.

Ian MacGregor saw the triumph against Wales as a victory for character and to this writer that applied especially to two of the Scottish backs for whom the match did not go uniformly well – John Rutherford and Peter Dods.

At the very height of his managerial renown, Jock Stein made a remark to me which I have never forgotten – that it is not so much the players in form who win you the critical matches but what you are getting from those a bit out of touch.

Rutherford epitomised that shrewd assertion against France. Even when unexpectedly at war with his kicking and with nothing going quite right for him, he never stopped competing in both attack and defence, tackling invaluably and all through posing enough of a threat to keep the French defence worrying.

It is no coincidence that the only other time Scotland won the Grand Slam they had a club partnership at half-back in Nelson and Waddell, a club partnership being what Laidlaw and Rutherford have virtually become. Nor, as Herbert Waddell himself was quick to endorse over breakfast on the morning of the French match, should anyone overlook the effect on Scotland's fortunes in the sixties of the telepathic understanding of Hastie and Chisholm.

There are days when Rutherford tends to crowd his centres a little, shuttle the ball on to them; days when he could do with more of the classic swing and rhythm of stand-offs of bygone decades as he sets his three-quarters running. But he was, without question, the key Scottish back in the Grand Slam. Whether he is at his best or not, there is always that unmistakable suggestion of class.

His kicking has improved dramatically over the years and his ability to beat a man, to slice open a defence, means that even when he is lying dormant he is always atracting the eye of the defence and, accordingly, easing the lot of others. In 1983, when he returned to the Scotland XV for the Calcutta Cup after injury, he at once split England open and Scotland suddenly looked an entirely different side from the team of earlier matches.

Dods has an ability to put mishaps behind him, be they missed goal-kicks or maybe a couple of untypical fielding lapses, reminiscent of Bobby Locke's ability in the sphere of golf to forget a bad start or a disastrous hole.

Of the penalty goals with which he failed, Dods's half-closed eye was watering before he missed the short one but, very likably, he doubted that his damaged eye had had anything to do with it: 'I think I just snatched at it as I did in Paris last year and it helped for the later ones that David Leslie said encouragingly, "Just calm down and take your time".'

When his boot split and his toes peeped out into the open air at Cardiff – which was scarcely the kind of advertisement on international day for which manufacturers were apparently not so long ago paying such sizeable sums of boot money – Dods banged over his goals unperturbed. But then temperament can be a funny thing . . .

There have been batsmen who found it relatively easier to make runs in Test cricket than on the county round. Without burdening Dods with any extreme claims at this juncture of his career, it was revealing to hear him reflect in the small hours of the night after the French match that he rather thought that so far he had found kicking goals somewhat easier in international rugby than back on the club scene.

Away from goal-kicking, Dods to me is a better player when he plays as Peter Dods rather than as Andy Irvine. Though he is no mean attacking player with his timely intrusions, he can be rather too readily consumed behind the gain line when he attempts to run the ball out of defence à la Irvine at his most electrifying.

There was, incidentally, a poignant moment on that last afternoon against France. Irvine, named as a replacement both against Ireland and France, not least as the goal-kicking cover for Dods which Scotland had lacked all season without being made to rue it, came as close to a fifty-second cap as to be sent to the back pitch at Murrayfield to warm up when Peter Dods and Roger Baird were injured.

Irvine, who announced his retirement from representative rugby the next day, confessed that he had experienced an eagerness and a tingle at the prospect of getting on to the field which he had not known for close on two years. There is no favourite like an old favourite and had he taken the field the roar would surely have matched those which greeted the Triple Crown heroes of Lansdowne Road when they took the field at Murrayfield and that which hailed the Grand Slam champions at no-side.

Jim Pollock's best moment remained the perceptive quick-thinking which saw him score from Johnston's oblique punt against the All Blacks, an equalising try which had not a little to do with the confidence with which Scotland thereafter played for the remainder of the season. As for Johnston, he takes the ball rather

Above The half-closed eye and battered countenance of Peter Dods as the full-back hammers into the shoulder charge of his French counterpart, Serge Blanco, with Jim Pollock in anxious supplication. *Bob Thomas*

Below John Rutherford, whose kicking repertoire was in telling evidence throughout the season, clips the ball past Jean-Luc Joinel. *Bob Thomas*

better than he gives it but his whiplash acceleration and willingness to tackle far above his weight were priceless ingredients.

He and Robertson, who has something of Iain Laughland's sheer footballing resource, disguised what was undeniably a certain lack of physical presence in midfield after the loss of Euan Kennedy – whom Derek Morgan, chairman of the England selectors, had described, with memorable hyperbole, after England's most promising attack had come down about his prone figure, as 'a seven-foot six-inch centre over whom we tripped'.

As that great prop of bygone days, Hawick's Hughie McLeod, was to observe, the public now have a better idea of what is happening when the halves are kicking for position or playing back to their forwards. For that understanding, of course, the game is indebted most to McLeod's world-famous fellow townsman, Bill McLaren, who, in addition to his intimate knowledge of the laws and powers of identification, has always been willing to risk the ire of the more knowledgeable in order to explain a point for what is by far the larger portion of his audience.

McLeod, in my opinion, stands out as the man who had the greatest influence on Scottish forward play in the post-war era for he instilled into Hawick what he had learned with the Lions in South Africa in 1955 and, to an even greater degree, in New Zealand in 1959.

Of course, it has been possible for the keener rugby men to supplement that knowledge in a variety of ways, not least through such books as *The Lions Speak* by John Reason and *How The Lions Won* by Terry O'Connor wherein some of the most celebrated Lions of the early seventies divulged their own rugby learning – but Hawick so bestrode the Scottish scene that it was McLeod's teaching that mainly affected the game in Scotland.

No one is likely to be in less danger than McLeod of failing to recognise the difference between a leading club side in Scotland's domestic rugby and the international arena. Nevertheless, he has made clear his view that in a game where Hawick, in winning the 1983–84 Schweppes Scottish Championship (and, for the record, providing Scotland with two new caps in Alister Campbell and the explosive young flanker, Sean McGaughey, who made his international debut versus Rumania), could score seventy-three tries and yield only three, it ought to be possible for Scotland to move towards a rather more flowing game than that which took them to their first Grand Slam in almost three score years.

Nowadays the Hawick President, McLeod has loomed large, in one way or another, in the careers of the three Hawick men who are now central to Scotland's immediate future – Robin Charters, the convener of the selectors, Colin Telfer, the Scotland coach who also happens to be McLeod's nephew, and Derrick Grant who will help Colin Telfer with the forwards as Colin helped Jim Telfer with the backs.

They take over against the background of a Grand Slam whereas the harsh realism of Jim Telfer's pragmatic approach, though natural to the man, might well have been adopted by many with more flamboyant leanings who had to take over a national side, as Jim Telfer did, which had won only two of their previous eighteen internationals.

No one will be hoping that the ball is spun rather more often more than Roger Baird who alone of the Grand Slam backs of 1984 has not scored a try for Scotland, a curious anomaly in a wing of his footballing attributes and of a pace which gave rise to the story most often retold of those already multiplying around the men of the Grand Slam: the story of how Borderers teased Roger Baird senior, a darned good player himself, that young Roger must have got his speed from his mother.

'Maybe so,' returned Roger Baird Mark I, 'but don't forget, I caught her!'

Final Table

	P	W	D	L	F	A	Pts
Scotland	4	4	0	0	86	36	8
France	4	3	0	1	90	67	6
Wales	4	2	0	2	67	60	4
England	4	1	0	3	51	83	2
Ireland	4	0	0	4	39	87	0

The Nine Crowns

1891	Wales 15–0 Raeburn Place	Ireland 14–0 Belfast	England 9–3 Richmond
1895	Wales 5–4 Raeburn Place	Ireland 6–0 Raeburn Place	England 6–3 Richmond
1901	Wales 18–8 Inverleith	Ireland 9–5 Inverleith	England 18–3 Blackheath
1903	Wales 6–0 Inverleith	Ireland 3–0 Inverleith	England 10–6 Richmond
1907	Wales 6–3 Inverleith	Ireland 15–3 Inverleith	England 8–3 Blackheath
1925	Wales 24–14 Swansea	Ireland 14–8 Dublin	England 14–11 Murrayfield
1933	Wales 11–3 Swansea	England 3–0 Murrayfield	Ireland 8–6 Dubliln
1938	Wales 8–6 Murrayfield	Ireland 23–14 Murrayfield	England 21–16 Twickenham
1984	Wales 15–9 Cardiff	England 18–6 Murrayfield	Ireland 32–9 Dublin

THE FRENCH SLANT

Bob Donahue

The Grand Slam match was the proverbial elephant that blind wisemen perceive very differently, depending on which part of the beast each sage happens to have examined. While Scots of all ages exulted, the French were angry; and French reactions themselves were various. 'So long as I live, I shall never forget the year 1984 when France were robbed and insulted at Murrayfield,' wrote a reader to the national sports daily *L'Equipe*. 'Scottish joy at achieving a long-awaited Grand Slam,' wrote another, 'was, oddly enough, our only consolation of the day.' Jean-Pierre Rives touched both these extremes of French reaction when he maintained that 'Scotland definitely deserved their Grand Slam,' yet, 'our feeling tonight is that of a side which lost without being beaten.'

'A very good side,' Rives later called the Scots. But that had been expected. French players had been saying for several seasons that Scotland played the best rugby in the British Isles. It was commonly held in France that Aitken's team had been unlucky to lose in Paris in 1983. By the simple measure of tries scored in the championship during the 1980s, Scotland and France entered 1984 neck-and-neck out in front (27 tries for Scotland in 16 matches, 26 tries for France) and together they steadily increased their lead over the three other nations so that at the end of the season it stood: Scotland 37 tries in 20 matches, France 35, Wales 28, England 24, Ireland 21. On the morning of the 1984 finale, *L'Equipe*'s premier rugby writer, Denis Lalanne, speculated that the French would be glad of a draw at Murrayfield.

One heard a bit of hopeful speculation that the Scots might have gone off the boil after the historic Triple Crown rout in Dublin. 'Rubbish,' said coach Fouroux. 'Scots haven't lacked motivation against us at Murrayfield when they were at the bottom of the Five Nations table, so you can imagine what they'll be like going for the Grand Slam!' He forecast that Edinburgh would prove 'even harder than Cardiff', where France's forwards were outplayed. Still, he expected an improved performance from an improved French pack. He seemed to partake of the general perception in France that Rives' team were riding an upward curve that ought to carry them through to the Grand Slam. His pre-match comment was realistic nevertheless.

'The scrummage will be the key to the match,' Fouroux forecast. The aim would be 'to dominate at forward without complexes.' He hoped France would just about hold their own in the line-outs despite the loss of Erbani – whom Lalanne, among others, had been calling France's best forward of the season. The late inclusion of Haget, further increasing the Scottish pack's advantage in mobility, made early and relentless scrummage domination all the more vital. ('Win the rucks in the scrum,' as someone put it.) By the same token, it increased the onus on France to build a comfortable early lead in the scoring. The fear, Fouroux would later admit, was that the big match would be lost in the last quarter for want of being won in the first. With luck, though, Scotland would have to scramble to catch up, the game would break open and France's superior back division would secure the victory. And thus it would be a great match.

But luck was certainly not with the French. Lopsided domination in the first half (fully a dozen French scoring opportunities, to only three for Scotland) netted an insignificant lead of six points to three. When Scotland drew even at 12–12, Haget felt in his weary bones that the match was lost. 'The Scots played exactly as I expected,' Fouroux said afterwards. 'I knew their only hope to score would be from up-and-unders and other kicks. They did what they had to do, and they did it well.'

Gallion's frightening departure was another part of the Murrayfield elephant. Like the French team doctor, several French players feared for a terrible moment that the fallen scrum-half was dead. Rives inserted fingers in his mouth to stop him strangling on his tongue. But 'we didn't lose because of the loss of Gallion,' Fouroux would say. 'We had let victory go begging while Gallion was still there.'

Scottish teamwork and fitness. The loss of Gallion, arguably the championship's outstanding player. Rives' reputation for influencing referees, which clearly inclined Winston Jones to greater severity towards the Frenchman (Rives was marched back ten metres on one occasion for a silent Gallic shrug) than towards the talkative gamesmanship of Aitken and Leslie. The disallowing of two apparent French tries. Scottish defence. Technical failings on France's right wing. Scottish home advantage. A French game-plan that shot too many cartridges too soon.

Of all the elephant's parts, the refereeing of Mr Jones was the hardest for Frenchmen to approve. A penalty free-kick count against France of eight to nil in the first quarter? 'We had thought of all the possibilities, we really thought of everything,' Joinel recalled, 'except one thing – a one-eyed referee.' *Midi Olympique*, the national rugby weekly, consulted all twelve of France's past and current international referees and obtained comment ranging from 'calamitous' (Robert Calmet) and 'gravely worrisome for the future of rugby' (Jacques Saint-Guilhem) to 'no comment' (Francis Palmade), but not a word of praise. Yet Fouroux, again: 'We weren't defeated by the referee. We beat ourselves.'

Fouroux singled out Paxton and Deans for special praise. *L'Equipe*'s nine rugby writers all picked Paxton and Aitken for the newspaper's Five Nations Best XV; Leslie received seven votes and Calder five, which made four Scots in the pack. *Midi Olympique* added Milne, making it five.

There was anger in France when the London press stressed Scottish character while mocking the French (the *Daily Telegraph*, for one, headlined: 'Character of Scots Upsets Silly French') – as if France hadn't shown notable character amid leagued adversities. But Fouroux observed: 'When all is said and done, maybe Scotland wanted victory even more than we did.'

6
Another Voice, Another Angle

by John Reason

William Shakespeare would have appreciated the irony of Scotland's emphatic defeat by Rumania at the game of rugby football in May 1984. After all, it was he who first crafted the expression 'Hoist with his own petard' into the English language.

For those, in these non-National Service days, with a depressingly scant knowledge of ordnance, or even of Shakespeare, perhaps it should be explained that, back in the Middle Ages, a petard was a crude explosive device for blasting an entrance into a fortification, and, sometimes, these things went off before they should have done.

Since then, of course, more prosaic organizations such as MI5 and the SAS have given us the even more succinct expression 'own goal' to describe what happens when someone trying to manipulate explosive devices succeeds in blowing himself up, and that expression will do just as nicely to explain what happened to Scotland in the year of our Lord 1984.

What happened was this. Scotland won the International Championship by doing nothing more ambitious than kicking the ball up in the air and running after it, and by enjoying socking great dollops of good fortune. When all that was over, Rumania beat Scotland by doing exactly the same thing.

As Bill McLaren lamented, 'Rumania just punted high and chased, and Scotland, short of ball, succumbed to a strategy simple, uncomplicated, effective and hard to break down.'

The only difference was that Rumania did not need any good fortune to beat Scotland, in the way of refereeing enormities, and, what is more, they had the grace afterwards to apologize for what they had done and the way they had done it. Their coach asked publicly, 'Is this what we want from rugby football?' He did not seek to justify the means by which Rumania had achieved their short-term end. By asking the question that he did, he indicated quite clearly that he was aware of the awful implications for the future if the way Rumania had played ever became standard practice.

The pity is that Shakespeare is not still around to put these events into perspective with an unforgettably devastating choice of words, because no one ever hit more nails more squarely on the head than the strolling player from Stratford on Avon. Rugby writing, in particular, could do with a couple or three like him at the moment.

Still, the bard did not do at all badly, because the beauty of his aphorism was that he reinforced it, back and front, with words which were just as much to the point.

'For 'tis the sport to have the engineer
Hoist with his own petard; and it shall go hard'

Indeed it is a sport. Indeed it did go hard. What is more, Shakespeare went on to say:

'But I will delve one yard below their mines,
and blow them at the moon.'

Which is where I come in. To delve, and to blow the Scots at the moon, and one or two more with them.

Scotland's success in the 1984 International Championship was the greatest disaster to befall British rugby and the game as a whole since the 1974 British Lions tour of South Africa. I had a few words to say about that, too, and its dreadful portents for the future, and I have lived to see every one of those words proved right, so, ten years on, I shall address myself to exactly the same threat with exactly the same determination.

The threat did not come only from Scotland, either, because quite the most depressing feature of the 1984 season in the Four Home Unions was that easily the most successful club side in terms of results in the big league was Pontypool, and easily the most successful international team was Scotland, and both played in exactly the same way. They both aspired to do nothing more risky than kick the ball up in the air and run after it.

Pontypool did it off a much more powerful forward base, and with a much more scientific analysis of the kicking percentages. Scotland simply ran after the ball quicker.

Since then, I have made this point over and over again to various conferences of coaches and at various club dinners in various parts of the world. I have said that it would be difficult to imagine any contest more tedious or more totally destructive of more than half the game's precepts than a match between Pontypool and Scotland. I have said – not from any sense of mischief, but from a realistic assessment of individual and corporate playing ability – that I think Pontypool would beat Scotland, particularly at Pontypool Park on a Wednesday night. I also think that Pontypool would beat Rumania.

David Bishop, the Pontypool scrum-half, was particularly amusing on the subject at the Hong Kong international sevens earlier in the year. So was John Robbie, the former Irish international scrum-half, when he sat on the replacement's bench for South Africa against England in June.

A few years ago, Robbie, then the captain of Cambridge University, was persuaded by his team-mate, Eddie Butler, to go down to Pontypool to play the remainder of a club season for them, and his account of the instructions he received from Ray Prosser, the legendary Pontypool coach, on the way the game should be played, ought to be included in every coaching manual and in every humorous book written about rugby.

David Bishop, with a delightfully sharp Welsh humour, supported every word that Robbie said, and so did Syd Millar, the Lions coach of 1974 and the Lions manager of 1980. Millar and Prosser toured New Zealand as props with the British Lions in 1959 and Syd said that, even then, Ray never believed in giving the backs the ball. 'They'll only drop it,' said he. As far as 'Pross' was concerned, giving the backs the ball was one of the seven deadly sins of rugby football, and when he became coach of Pontypool, he worked out by hard and practical experience just where the ball should be kicked and how high it should be kicked and at what angle it should be kicked, from every position on the field. There was a carefully calculated target area for every type of ball received by the scrum-half for every position on the field in which he found himself. Furthermore, the other fourteen players in the team all knew exactly where the ball would be kicked. Even ten yards from the opposing line, the alternatives were chips or grubbers or diagonals or up-and-unders – but no passes, except inside to the loose forwards, or when watching 'Mastermind'.

Bishop said that when he joined Pontypool, and Prosser introduced him to his fly-half, he said, 'And that's the nearest you're going to so-and-so well get to him for the rest of the so-and-so time you are at this club.'

Scotland were nothing like as calculating or as efficient as Pontypool at kicking the ball up in the air and running after it, because they have been doing it for nothing like as long, and they have not thought about it nearly as deeply, but that is what they did in 1984, and, in the delightfully exact soccer parlance of the day, it got them four results. In the cringingly inadequate rugby parlance of the day, it also got them a Grand Slam, though if ever two words in conjunction were utterly debased, those two were by what Scotland did.

Accordingly, the words spoken by Valeriu Irimescu, the coach of Rumania, after his team had got their result against Scotland came as the scent of roses in the summer air. 'Is this really what we want from rugby?' he asked. Then he answers himself. 'Surely not. We must expand our game. We must develop our backs as an attacking force.'

Mircea Paraschiv, his captain and scrum-half, had said exactly the same thing to me after France had demolished Rumania in Toulouse in December 1983. 'I want to become a coach, and to coach Rumania to better things,' he said. 'We must end our obsession with kicking. It is easy – too easy – to gain ground by doing that, but, if we go on, we will end up playing in an empty stadium.'

Unfortunately, that will not happen in Scotland, because the rugby public at Murrayfield is one of the least discriminating in the world. To them, only the end matters, not the means, and to make matters worse, they are not only the worst losers in the world, but the worst winners, too. The threats of physical violence offered to Jean-Pierre Rives, the French captain, in the North British Hotel after Scotland's match against France in 1984 were absolutely disgraceful. 'Stitch that, Jimmy' after a head-butt may be par for the course on the soccer grounds of Glasgow, but you can only weep for a community – I was going to say 'sporting' community, but changed my mind – which offers to do that in relation to rugby football.

The game between Scotland and France, of course, was the one which ultimately decided the International Championship, and I will go to my grave with my head bowed in the certainty that I contributed to the appalling injustice of the day. I had written that it really was time that the French forwards were refereed in the line-out, and I went on to say something laudatory about the leading Welsh referees. In writing that, it never occurred to me that the referee in question, Winston Jones, would concentrate so hard on that particular aspect that he would ignore completely the basis of Scotland's spoiling game, which was for their flankers and their midfield to be as far off-side for as much of the time as they possibly could, knowing that France would try to play football, and that Scotland would not. The result was that France were refereed and Scotland were not.

It was Winston Jones' first international refereeing appointment, and, as Norman Sanson, the distinguished former Scottish international referee, said before the game, it was both unfair and unrealistic to appoint a man making his debut to a game of such reverberating importance. This view was substantiated by what happened on the day, and it persuaded France to propose that international refereeing appointments should be made as the season progresses so that games of such importance as to decide a Triple Crown or a Grand Slam should only be given to the best and most experienced of referees.

Clive Norling, whom I rate as probably the best referee in the world at the moment, was one of the Welsh touch judges that day, and I have no doubt that, if he had refereed the game, France would have won it by twenty points. Any acknowledgement of justice demanded that they should.

France had their weaknesses, heaven knows. The previous December, when the rest of the world were throwing their caps over the moon about their performance against Rumania, I was the only one to point out that the French forwards, without Paparemborde and Dospital, were anything but impressive. But from every point of view – justice, quality, ability – France deserved twenty points for the first half they played against Scotland. They got six, and incipient apoplexy. With Norling in charge, I am sure they would have scored those twenty points and developed the sense of well-being which comes from skilful adventure rewarded.

In the end, the French felt, and I felt, and some extremely distinguished observers felt, that France had been refereed out of it. The French blew their tops. Jean-Pierre Rives lost his cool. Scotland got their result and got their Grand Slam.

Well, there is a corner of Murrayfield that I thought belonged forever to a certain Welsh referee under whose jurisdiction Scotland rarely failed to prosper. He and his wife still go to Scotland for their holidays. In 1985, he could find that he has been evicted. Winston Jones will get the lot, including the Freedom of the City.

You see, the curious thing is that none of the international players who played against Scotland in 1984 were impressed by them. The only two players in the Scottish team for whom any of the other countries would have given more than tuppence-ha'penny were David Leslie and Jim Calder.

John Rutherford, whose kicking meant so much to Scotland. *Dave Stranock*

It has to be admitted that they, and Wales in particular, would have given quite a few bob for David Leslie, but even that says something two-edged about the development of the game, because the last two years has seen flankers exerting a disturbingly disproportionate influence on the play at international level. But that is another matter and another article at another time.

David Leslie has had a strange career. He should have been on at least two Lions tours but missed one when he seemed uncertain as to whether he wanted to go, missed another through injury and missed a third because he was not selected. Jim Telfer, Scotland's coach, was also the Lions coach when Leslie was not selected, and I understand that they have never exactly been the president of each other's fan clubs. Whatever the truth of the matter, Leslie certainly played like a tiger for Scotland and for Telfer in 1984.

But to get back to the players' opinions of Scotland. The Welsh believe, as Malcolm Dacey said, that they could and should have won all four matches that they played. I do not subscribe entirely to that view because Wales have a horrible void at scrum-half if Terry Holmes is not fit, and they are still a long way adrift with their selections at loose forward, but, against that, Wales only lost to Scotland because of refereeing mistakes.

Again, Owen Doyle, the Irish referee in question, was having his first match at international level at what looked like a rather late stage in his career, and he missed two forward passes in the move from which Scotland scored the try which won the match. This sort of thing really does make a nonsense of international rugby.

When England were at Peebles preparing for their Calcutta Cup match against Scotland, one of their most experienced backs said of the morrow's opponents, 'Look at them. What have they got? The full-back drops the ball. So do both the wingers. There isn't a convincing tackler between the three of them and one of the centres doesn't like tackling, either. The other centre can't turn. You know just what Roy Laidlaw is going to do. John Rutherford is a tidy player, but he has been having a bad season. What is more, they all know that we played a much better game against the All Blacks than they did. We ought to be giving them the run around, but I don't suppose we will. We'll manage to make a cock-up somewhere.'

This rueful analysis proved accurate in every detail. England had the chances in the first half hour to give Scotland the run around, but did not take them, and in the process they managed to play Rutherford back into form. This was crucial. But after the match

ANOTHER VOICE, ANOTHER ANGLE

England were convinced that they had given the game away. They were uncomfortably aware that two of their forwards should not have played because of lack of fitness, but their view of Scotland's players had not changed by one iota. Certainly, there was no feeling whatever that England had been overcome by a force of any significance in international rugby. It was just seen as yet another English muddle.

Even the Irish were no more flattering, and, if you except their press, who go through the worst-losers tape with the multitude at Murrayfield, the Irish are easily the most gracious at both winning and losing in the whole wide world of international rugby. In no other country would it be possible for two international teams to share the same hotel and never fail to get along exceedingly well.

Anyway, speaking on the night before Ireland played Scotland in Dublin, Fergus Slattery, Ireland's immensely experienced former captain, said, 'If Scotland are down at half-time, even by as little as nine points, they will find it difficult to cope with the pressure. They will tighten up. They will try too hard. They will press; make mistakes. In that situation, I would not fancy them at all. But Ireland have to get in among them before they can settle down.'

As Slattery spoke, a gale was howling outside, and the gale kept blowing throughout the next day. Straight down Lansdowne Road. Just what Ireland were praying for, particularly if they could win the toss. There is no greater disrupter of a game of football than a wind; nothing which enables spoilers to prosper more readily. And the Lord be praised, Ireland DID win the toss.

So what did Willie Duggan do, as Ireland's new captain? He gave Scotland first use of the gale. He gave the Scots a twenty points start. He let the Scots gorge themselves at the feast while Ireland waited outside the door. He settled the Scots' nerves. He boosted their confidence so high that by half-time they might just as well have been on LSD. In one sense, of course, they were. On pounds, shillings and pence. They laughed all the way to the bank. Dublin could not believe it. Neither could Belfast. Neither could anyone else. It was one of the most extraordinary captaincy decisions in post-war international rugby. Presumably, it must have been taken in conjunction with Ireland's coach, Bill McBride. Maybe it helped to explain why, at the end of the season, McBride was replaced as Ireland's coach after only one year in the job.

The Irish, being the Irish, just shrugged and smiled and said to the Scots, 'Good luck to you.' What is more, they meant it. But

87

the Irish knew, as everyone else knew, that they had given the game away.

So Scotland ended up by winning four matches in which they convinced no one except their supporters that they were much of a team at all, and, having played the way they did, it was easy to understand why Jim Renwick holds the view he does of playing for Scotland under the coaching of Jim Telfer. It would have been interesting to see what Andy Irvine would have made of it if he had been available for selection.

Back in 1974, Andy Irvine had been a young Lion in South Africa who, for a long time, felt that he ought to be loyal to the 'scrummage-and-kick and hang the back-play' ethic which the British Lions used to win the series. These tactics seemed to me to be unnecessary because the Lions were playing such a disorganized Springbok team that they were in effect playing the blind school, but what was of even greater concern to me was that such a playing policy would obviously be technically and aesthetically destructive to the future of British back-play. I was in a minority of one when I pointed out that, if we went on like that, then in ten years' time we would have no backs left.

When 1984 eventually came around, of course, British back-play had deteriorated to such an extent that there was not one world-class player to be found anywhere in the Four Home Unions, and that after three-quarters of a century when we never had anything less than an entire back division. The only possible exception might have been Terry Holmes because even on one leg he towered above his rivals, but in such a dubious state of fitness I doubt if even he would have been able to hold off the scrum-half challenge of Dave Loveridge and Jerome Gallion.

It ought to go without saying that in 1974 I was arguing for the future of players like Andy Irvine. I do not expect he was old enough or wise enough to know what I was up to at the time, but by the end of that tour even Irvine was beginning to develop doubts about what the Lions were doing. He turned to Mike Gibson and said, 'I wonder if John Reason might not be right after all.'

Now it is my turn to wonder whether any of the current crop of Scottish backs have the sense to be able to look through their dark blue spectacles, beyond the brick wall of the kick and chase rugby they have been playing, and ask themselves if this is what they really want. Is this really the rugby they believe in? Do they really think it is going to do anything but harm to the future of the game in Scotland and anywhere else daft enough to use it as a national prototype?

Grand Slams notwithstanding, as far as European international rugby in 1984 was concerned, the best value by far were France and Wales. The other four countries – you have to include Rumania now – were nowhere. If the international game in Europe has any future, it has to lie in France and Wales.

Is it a coincidence that France and Wales were coached by backs, and that England, Scotland and Ireland were coached by forwards? I doubt it. This is another argument which I have been making since 1974. It is too easy to coach forwards. Indeed, the 1977 Lions forwards in New Zealand coached themselves, and they destroyed the All Blacks' pack to such an extent that they reduced them to three-man scrums. But the poverty of the Lions' back-play was such that they could not turn that massive forward superiority into a victory in the series. As Fran Cotton said when he walked out to the aircraft when the Lions left Auckland, 'I just don't believe it.' The Lions were beaten, and beaten hollow, in the backs, and that was only three years after what had happened in South Africa in 1974.

The same thing happened in South Africa in 1980 when the Lions' management and captaincy consisted of three forwards. The same thing happened again in New Zealand in 1983, when exactly the same forward combination was in command.

This is why the emergence of John Bevan as coach of Wales is so important to British rugby. He has picked a running back division of young players, and he has stuck to them. Either he or his fellow selectors are hopelessly wrong about his back row, but at least let us be grateful for the huge mercies which the new Welsh attitude will bestow upon our back-play.

Let us be grateful, too, for the change of heart of Valeriu Irimescu. I have known him for years as a friend, and indeed he asked me to give Rumania their team-talk in the dressing-room before they played Scotland at Murrayfield in 1981. I declined the invitation on the grounds of ethics, but I have to admit that I was tempted, if only to see the expression on the face of the liaison officer of the Scottish Rugby Union!

After that match, I talked at length with Valeriu Irimescu and with Viorel Morariu, the Rumanian manager. I said that as Rumania's game consisted solely of goal-kicking, of massive touch-kicking and of their scrum-half and captain, Mircea Paraschiv, either running or linking with his loose forwards, they were cutting off at least an arm and a leg from the body of their game, as well as any contact with their literally romantic roots.

My criticisms went back to Paraschiv, and he discussed them

with me after France had crushed Rumania two years later. It was then that Paraschiv said that he felt that Rumania must expand their game, or see it wither and die, and he wanted to become a coach to help them do it.

Then, after Rumania beat Scotland in 1984, Irimescu returned to the same theme. 'We must expand our game,' he said. 'We must convince our clubs to change their attitude. We have decided not to choose players from clubs who oppose the idea of open play. This will force those clubs to develop their three-quarters.

'If they won't change their attitude, they won't be given permission to tour abroad, or to play foreign teams in Rumania. It is that simple. We know that unless we can add some flair to the ability of our forwards, there is not much hope for us in international rugby.'

Irimescu also made the criticisms of Paraschiv that I did, while echoing my acknowledgement of his ability. 'He always looks to see if there is anything on for him as a scrum-half before he passes,' he said. 'By the time he does pass, it is either too late or much more difficult for his backs.'

Well, I can only say, 'Better late than never.' I hope the same light dawns in Scotland. The trouble is that Albert Ferrasse, the formidable president of France, cannot influence the Scots in the same way that he can influence the Rumanians. Ferrasse was as scathing about Rumania's attitude to rugby in 1983 as he was about some of the refereeing suffered by France in 1984 – and Ferrasse was a top-class player and referee himself. Ferrasse is the Godfather of European, that is, FIRA, rugby and when he says something categoric, Rumania takes notice.

I only wish that Ferrasse had the same sort of influence in the Five Nations. The emergence of a marvellously entertaining and successful French soccer team has left French rugby in no doubt that kicking the ball up in the air and running after it would empty Parc de Princes quicker than you can say Mitterand.

Backs, by their very nature, are delicate flowers. They have to be encouraged. They have to be nurtured. They have to be understood. It is this final consideration which fills me with such a dreadful sense of forboding about the success of Scotland. We have neither encouraged backs nor nurtured them nor understood them for ten years, and if kicking the ball up in the air and running after it is to be the totality of our ambitions then we might as well all go home.

I know that Pontypool were up to exactly the same thing as the Scots last season and that they were doing it better, but as a club they were only providing their national selectors with a choice; providing them with some truly battle-hardened forwards; with some half-backs who could fill a very specific function. They were also providing other clubs with a genuine yardstick against which to measure themselves.

But Pontypool are not in the image-making game. They are not in the public relations game. They are not concerned with the national education and the national inspiration of the young. Scotland are concerned with all three, or at any rate, they ought to be.

Oddly enough, Jim Telfer allowed his backs to express themselves when he started as Scotland's coach. Indeed, I can remember how surprised I was when he told me that the nature of his squad of backs was such that he felt he had to let them do their thing. 'Leopards can't change their spots,' he said.

Now Jim's rugby faith as a player was as puritanical as sack-cloth and about as pretentious. He was one of the most destructive loose forwards I have seen and was prepared to take any amount of punishment, without complaining, to do it. When he became captain of Scotland, his brows would beetle and thunder at even the slightest evidence of play which resembled what R. H. Williams once forbiddingly referred to as 'That 'Arlem Globetrotters stuff.' As captain of Scotland, one of Jim Telfer's most favoured comments to his backs was, 'Don't ever do that again, son.'

So to see Jim Telfer crinkle his eyes and smile and shrug and be philosophical about the importance of allowing his backs to whizz about a bit was an event which startled me, and, after all these years, I can tell you that JR does not startle easily.

But as Jim said, leopards do not change their spots, and, after the disasters of the British Lions tour of New Zealand in 1983 when, as coach, he attempted so much that was unrealistic and which made no sense at all in view of the disposition of the forces available to the two teams, he decided to clap his Quaker's hat back on his head and to beetle and thunder away.

His team-talks must have been a Border country translation of Ray Prosser's, without the expletives. His backs must have been made to stand with their hands on a thistle and promise to stick faithfully to the kick, the whole kick and nothing but the kick. His flankers and midfield must have promised to devote themselves to the off-side, the whole off-side and nothing but the off-side, and what was even more surprising was that most (though not quite all) of his backs must also have promised to commit themselves to the tackle, the whole tackle and nothing but the tackle.

As I say, with the help of Winston Jones, the Welsh selectors, Owen Doyle, Willie Duggan and the entire England team, the roulette wheel produced four wins from four spins, but God help rugby football if it ever happens in those circumstances again.

The only glimmer of light and hope which has come from North of the Border since those awful events in the first three months of 1984 has been an interview with Hugh McLeod, the president of Hawick, which I read recently. Hugh McLeod also toured New Zealand with the British Lions as a prop in 1959 and literally stood shoulder to shoulder with Syd Millar and Ray Prosser. The difference was that Hugh McLeod also had the priceless advantage of having toured South Africa with that wonderful running Lions team in 1955 and there he was, bless his soul, saying 'Most of our games are dominated by the boot. We kick so much ball away that the number of our actual handling movements are few and far between. How can a wing be expected to take a difficult pass if it is the only one he gets in the whole game?

'I would love to see John Rutherford run more. He has it in him to take people on and to create space for others. We do not encourage enough our gifted players to trust their own instinct and judgement in spinning the ball.'

Hugh McLeod, bless his soul, is concerned that much of the rugby football he saw in 1983–84 was not attractive enough. Well, he could not have been talking about his club, because they won the Scottish club championship by taking people on and scoring tries all over the place. Was he talking about Scotland? I hope so. Oh, how I hope so.

7
___A Players' Game___

Players are apt to have a rooted contempt for the middle-aged or older adolescent still trying desperately to be 'one of the boys'. But, without being in any danger of succumbing to that pitfall, the Scottish selectors in 1984 gave more signs of being on the same wavelength as the players than one had known before.

It helped, of course, that the two coaches, Jim and Colin Telfer, were on the selection committee. That was an advantage Nairn MacEwan enjoyed but not Bill Dickinson who, to be honest, sometimes struck one as being closer to the players than he was to the selectors.

There was, though, a great deal more to it than merely the inclusion of the coaches on the selection committee. In the past the players would wink ruefully at each other as, for the umpteenth time at some rugby dinner, they heard yet another alickadoo profess devoutly that it was a players' game; but it is a phrase to which Ian MacGregor and his co-selectors paid much more than simply lip service.

Indeed, by way of a prelude to the campaign which ended in the Grand Slam, MacGregor and Colin Telfer had an informal lunch with the side's 'senior pros' at which those longer-serving players were invited to give vent to their views on the various little things off the field and in terms of preparation which can make such a difference.

'Ian MacGregor,' remarked Jim Telfer one night in mid-championship, 'has worked his butt off on behalf of the players and has done a better job behind the scenes in terms of organization than many would appreciate.'

There are several reasons why Scotland's results away from home have improved, with five triumphs already in the Eighties against two in the whole of the 1970s. Yet the practice of taking the team away from the town centres to a quiet retreat where they can prepare properly is not the least of them and it is something MacGregor wanted from the day he took over.

From their base in the neighbouring foothills, Kilternan, the players emerged to slaughter Ireland and to put in an appearance at the post-match dinner before returning in the night to their lair. It gave to the whole thing the air of, as Jim Telfer put it memorably, 'an SAS strike'.

MacGregor reckoned Telfer at once 'straightforward, yet complex,' and he will tell you that the team were forged out of many a fierce head-to-head argument.

Relatively seldom, however, had the selection committee of MacGregor, the two Telfers, Robin Charters and Bob Munro actually had to vote to settle a difference of opinion. Only once, to the best of MacGregor's recollection, had Jim Telfer had a player who might not have been his choice had it been left to him alone and even then he was not sufficiently disturbed to preclude a gruff, 'Fair enough.'

Contemporary with Hamish Kemp in the Glasgow Schools XV, MacGregor packed down at lock with him at senior district level and actually played a national trial in that berth. Nevertheless, it was as a harshly abrasive flanker that this former pupil of Hillhead High School came into a Scotland team which, in 1955, would almost certainly have won the Triple Crown had not a try by Tom Elliot been controversially disallowed.

MacGregor took over from Bill Glen, who lost his place through injury after having won his only cap in 'Arthur Smith's match', the victory over Wales at Murrayfield which ended the infamous run of 17 successive defeats. In all, MacGregor won nine caps before an arthritic ankle spelt the end of his playing career, with two wins out of two against France among his battle laurels.

A member of an RAF side which lost only one match, to the Navy, in all the time he was with them, he played for Llanelli, who paid him the signal tribute for a Welsh club, who do not bestow such honours lightly, of making him captain against Bridgend for his farewell match.

The outstanding England flanker of the Fifties, Peter Robbins, remembers him as rugged and effective. The wonderfully gifted Oxford University and Welsh scrum-half, Onllwyn Brace, who played against him for Wales but never with him for Llanelli, deemed him a 'tigerish flanker' and added that he could think of an awful lot more comfortable things to do in life than go down on the ball at his feet.

As convener of the selectors, MacGregor was more than a little irritated that Roy Laidlaw's injury at Lansdowne Road had been widely misrepresented.

'Roy,' he explained, 'had blurred vision, a headache and some sickness but there was no confusion or loss of memory and it was certainly not concussion within the proper definition of that word.

'Actually it was something they call in American football, "footballer's migraine", a condition apparently brought on not just by the kind of knock Roy got in the vicinity of head and neck but by the tension to which a player is strung up for the great occasion.

'A brain scan showed no brain damage, either from the knock sustained at Lansdowne Road or previously, and no one should forget that we have a first-class medical team who would always ensure the best specialist advice. However keen we might have been to beat France and complete the Grand Slam, it annoyed me that anyone could think we would play with a young man's future.

'You wouldn't do that to one of your family and, without wanting to sound too fulsome, a family is very close to what this Scotland squad became.'

8
The Zealot

Ten times captain of Scotland in the days before there was even 'an adviser to the captain', Jim Telfer was often, as Ian McLauchlan appreciatively and shrewdly remarked, 'captain, coach and manager all in one.'

The style is the man and the same willingness, even urge, to drive himself to the limits is evident in his everyday life.

Last winter, he combined his duties as the Scotland coach with a schedule which had him leaving Selkirk at seven a.m. to be in school as deputy headmaster of Deans Community High School in Livingston, fifty-five miles away, and, at the weekend and sometimes in the evening, helping out in the bar of the Glen, his hotel in Selkirk. The school facilities remain open in the evening and once a week Telfer would not be heading back home until ten o'clock at night.

In Scotland it used to be said affectionately of Alf Wilson, the peppery manager of the 1959 Lions, not only that he had the courage of his own convictions rather than someone else's but that he could never be accused of being two-faced because, even given the richness of the resources of the English language, there was no way he could possibly be ruder behind your back than he was to your face.

Two-faced officials have been the pet hate of most players down the years and his own brand of harsh integrity has predictably stood Telfer in good stead. I have known him since he stood framed in the doorway of the changing-room at Goldenacre, a somewhat narrow-shouldered seventeen-year-old about to play a blinder in a resounding and highly improbable win for an understrength Melrose. Not everyone sees the same person in the same way but, to my eye, in good times and bad, he has always been his own man and absolutely straight.

A man's politics are his own business but suffice to say that

Your country needs you . . . Jim Telfer MBE in his most adamant
'Scotland expects' coaching vein. *Bob Thomas*

though Jim Telfer has mellowed with the years – if mellowed is a permissible word in such a context – one would still be very surprised if even now he were ever to take up an appointment in education's independent sector.

Nevertheless, Jack Dun, the erstwhile Melrose scrum-half who has known Telfer since he was a stripling, made a very pertinent point when he observed, 'Telfer might hate me for saying it but actually he has a lot in common with the public school tradition.'

Dun was not suggesting that such qualities were the exclusive preserve of the public schools, far from it. Merely that loyalty and discipline, hard work and uncomplaining courage in the face of adversity – none of which even Telfer's most vehement detractors would ever deny he possessed – were precisely the qualities the public schools used to pride themselves on inculcating into their charges from the days of Dr Arnold and before.

Kipling's *If* may have become a cliché but Telfer's bearing on his return home from the 1983 Lions tour of New Zealand, in which all four Tests were lost, put one irresistibly in mind of the lines:

> If you can make one heap of all your winnings
> And risk it on one turn of pitch-and-toss,
> And lose and start again at your beginnings
> And never breathe a word about your loss . . .

He never attempted to get out from under, blame anyone but himself. Neither, though, did he attempt to disguise the hurt. After Scotland had drawn 25–25 with the All Blacks at Murrayfield in November 1983, he was asked at the post-match press conference if the result in any way made up for what had happened to the Lions in New Zealand. 'Nothing,' he said, 'can ever make up for that.'

Twenty-five times capped for Scotland and eight times a Test player, Telfer – whose nickname of Creamy derived from a boyhood craze for a local horse which ran in the Grand National, Cream of the Border – was schooled in the game at the prolific rugby nursery of Galashiels Academy. The rugby master, Jim Shearer, had been a considerable player in his own right and Telfer recalls that, when Melrose dropped him in that first season as a seventeen-year-old, Shearer greeted this end-of-the-world calamity with a nod and 'That's probably the best thing that could happen.'

In all, Telfer played seventeen seasons for Melrose and was twice in sides which won the unofficial Scottish club championship. In six of his seasons he was captain, while the greatest of his many days in a South jersey surely came in 1969 when the Springboks were held to a 3–3 draw at Netherdale. The game was made all the more memorable by the superlative display of Peter Brown who cut the ball out of the air at the line-out in a manner entirely befitting the son of Jock Brown the international goalkeeper.

It used to be said that in the land of the Silver Fern not even Sir Winston Churchill was more vividly remembered as an orator than Jim Telfer. 'I am not going to say today's game was dirty,' quoth Telfer, at the post-match dinner after he had captained the Lions to victory over Canterbury in 1966, 'because every match in which I have played in New Zealand has been dirty.'

His words reverberated throughout the country, but there were some New Zealanders who came to his support, while even those who took umbrage had to admit that these were the words not of a squealer but of a man who played his rugby with a fearless commitment and selflessness very much after their own heart.

In truth, Telfer's own thinking has been mainly influenced by the All Blacks, partly because they are of much the same stock as ourselves, partly because they play in roughly the same conditions, but mostly because they have been so much more on the scene over the last decade and a half than those other major recipients of Lions tours, the Springboks.

By last season he had reached the stage in his career where, though still mindful of the fact that no one ever knows it all, he did feel that his own philosophy of the game had fully evolved.

The Lion trainer and his cubs. The Scottish contingent on the 1983 Lions tour with (left to right) Jim Telfer, John Rutherford, Roger Baird, John Beattie, Roy Laidlaw, Iain Milne, Colin Deans, Iain Paxton, Jim Calder and the team's honorary surgeon, Donald Macleod. *Bob Thomas*

Fundamentally, he wanted aggressive forward play with dynamic driving and rucking and with as much ball-playing athleticism as was available within the other physical requirements of a properly equipped international pack. Though that concept owed most to the All Blacks he would, ideally, have wished to complement such forward play with a back division reflecting the quick passing of the Wallabies and much of their thinking in terms of alignment and running on to the pass.

'Obviously,' he said, shortly before the Irish match, 'we are much closer to my ideal up front than we are behind, but you have to fit your game-plan and style to the best players on tap at the given time.'

He was well aware that many thought it ironic that a player who had often been castigated for killing rucks should emerge as the ruck's arch-apostle but, though he simply shrugged his shoulders and got on with it, he did privately consider that the criticism required some qualification.

Not that he had never killed a ruck – not remotely – but rather that time and again when he had gone down on the ball and laid the initial rampart, the packs in which he played at club and representative level had not been good enough or strong enough to drive over him. Thus a potentially productive ruck was rendered stillborn or, if the opposition were a pack like Hawick, as Telfer remembers ruefully but admiringly, he was heeled out with the ball.

Some of those pundits who argue that a back can never coach forwards properly or vice versa never let their own particular position on the field in their playing days stop them from pronouncing authoritatively on all fifteen berths and the most intimate technical and tactical aspects thereof.

That said, there are unquestionably many coaches who are better with the forwards than they are with the backs or the other way round and Telfer, to me, was best cast as the coach in overall command but with an assistant coach such as Colin Telfer to help him with the backs. Irrespective of how Colin Telfer fares as Jim Telfer's successor, no one should under-estimate his contribution to the Grand Slam. Certainly Jim Telfer never would.

Partly because they knew that he would never ask them to do anything he would not have done himself, most of the Scotland players would have followed Jim Telfer to hell and back. But it was said that when the England party, on tour in America, heard that Jim Telfer was to be the Lions coach, one player actually declared that in that case he was not going, because he had heard

Above Jim Aitken, Iain Milne and Colin Deans (from left to right) keep an additionally protective eye on Roy Laidlaw as the Scotland scrum-half serves his backs from behind an impenetrable Scottish security screen.
George Herringshaw

Below In the contemporary game, backs have an important part to play in the second phase. Here John Rutherford feeds the ball back from a skeletal maul to Roy Laidlaw with Colin Deans the alternative recipient. *Bob Thomas*

such daunting stories of the fiercely committed Telfer's long and gruelling training sessions and aversion to days off.

Aside from the fact that that player, if I deduced his identity correctly, was in the Lions party, Telfer came to appreciate the necessity of pacing the proceedings, of making sure that the players did not leave their strength behind on the training field as some allege had happened before Scotland's 40–15 defeat by the All Blacks at Auckland in the Second Test in 1981. But one suspects that terminating practices and deciding on days off never came easily to him.

Married with a fourteen-year-old son, Mark, and a thirteen-year-old daughter, Louise, he took the game home with him in the sense that he would spend many hours studying television recordings of past matches on the SRU video. 'I didn't watch the video latterly as much as I once did,' he explained, 'but I still found it helpful to see, for example, why penalties were given away and the technical points involved in the various ploys of ourselves and our opponents.'

As he came to realize that not everyone was made like him, or had his insatiable appetite for anything appertaining to the playing of the game, so he cut down on the video sessions for the players. Last season the most he would ask them to watch at one sitting was one half of a match, 'though by the time we got to the game itself, we would normally have seen the whole of our last match and the whole of the opposition's.'

Contrary to the impression many had, Jim Telfer had something of Carwyn James in him in that he was a good listener and, though he always had a mind of his own, he was generously quick to acknowledge to other people the source of a successful idea when it had not been his. He learned from defeat as well as victory and was quick to remind one that Melrose were relegated before coming back up when he was their coach and that he was on the wrong end of some agonizingly close results when he was doing the job for the South.

There was a touch of the Calvinist zealot about his approach to rugby while his forefathers had been Border shepherds and much of their hardiness was in him. As a player he had done better than many perhaps more richly endowed by making the very most of what he had got and that, basically, was what he sought to do with Scotland.

Many of the Grand Slam squad had been with him in the Scotland B team which he coached from 1974 until he took over as the full Scotland coach in 1981. Though he has said that it was not until his recent appointment as headmaster of Hawick High School that he finally and irrevocably decided to demit office, he had opined in mid-championship that he felt that he had probably taken the squad as far as they could go with him and that, as new players began to infiltrate the ranks, they would be all the better for a fresh voice.

To no small extent, it had become his team and Ian MacGregor, convener of the selectors, summed it up succinctly on the eve of the Irish match: 'The players are determined to give the man what he deserves and that, at the very least, is the Triple Crown.'

9
Ascent to Glory

A feet-on-the-ground realist in so many ways, Jim Aitken, through the lazy, hazy days of the summer of 1984, has worn the look of a Walter Mitty who has awoken from his daydreams to find that his headiest fantasies have come true.

Not capped until he was twenty-nine – admittedly in a berth, prop forward, where the occupants, like wines, are best allowed to mature – he had been discarded twice and retired once. Yet, in July, he found himself summoned to the Palace of Holyrood House, along with his wife, to sit down to dinner as a national hero with the Queen, the Duke of Edinburgh and Princess Anne, not to mention such lesser luminaries as the Duchess of Gloucester and the Secretary of State for Scotland.

Years ago, at a garden party at Holyrood, the Queen hove to opposite the late Arthur Smith, captain of Scotland and the 1962 Lions, and David Rollo, the indomitable prop who at one time, with forty caps, shared with the legendary Hughie McLeod the distinction of being Scotland's most capped player. Besides showing an unexpected rapport with such rugby brethren and listening cheerfully to a homely diatribe from Rollo, which must have come close to landing the Minister of Agriculture and Fisheries in the Tower, she remarked memorably that if her aides and advisors simply set her down at Twickenham without informing her where she was, the merest glance at the crowd would be sufficient to tell her.

At Holyrood, Royalty similarly impressed Aitken by their familiarity with Scotland's deeds over the past season while Princess Anne was soon busy comparing with Aitken his experiences in Rumania as a rugby player with those she had herself known behind the Iron Curtain as a showjumper. There might be a tiara or two between them but the Borderer was soon marvelling at the common bond among sportsmen, especially at international level.

There were many times in Aitken's career when captaining Scotland to a Triple Crown and Grand Slam had seemed light-years away; most notably when, having played flank forward for Penicuik High School First XV, he turned his back on the game and instead took to, ironically, the realm of the aforesaid Princess Anne, horse-riding.

The suspicion is that thereby he indirectly did his rugby career a heap of good for it was through that pastime that he met Ruth, the lady who was destined to become his wife and prove so steadfast in support of his eventual sporting outlet.

Returning to the rugby fold, he played as a flanker for Penicuik, turning out for the Edinburgh District XV in junior representative rugby and picking up, as he recalls, 'Something in the region of thirty tries a season.'

Billy Easson, the diminutive Gala midfield back who had been a prolific goal-kicker for Gala and no mean exponent of sevens, had come to live in Penicuik and, as Aitken puts it, 'He is one of those blokes who can spot a mile away whether a player can make the transition to higher things.'

Gala in modern times have seen themselves as an open club in the manner of, such as, Cardiff in Wales or Leciester in England. They have taken in their stride and mainly in good part such humorous barbs as that contained in the tale I first heard from Bill McLaren of the Gala supporter who, noting the presence of Colin Gass in the Hawick ranks, observed to a Hawick follower, 'I see you've got a Gala man playing for you today.'

'I see,' retorted the other, 'you've got one too!'

It was in 1971 that Aitken moved to Gala and, as befits one now steeped in the maroon hue, he talks not of 1971 as such but of 'the season Scotland beat England twice in eight days with six Gala men in the side!'

When a delegate from Gala, Frank Entwistle, had come to offer a second opinion on Easson's discovery, the day Penicuik were playing Preston Lodge, Aitken had played most of the game at prop because of an injury to the original incumbent and Entwistle had confirmed Easson's view that it was in that role that Aitken's future with Gala was likely to lie. However, Aitken made his debut at No. 8 for Gala A, alias the Gala Second XV, and, versus Gala YM, nabbed a try.

After three matches for the Seconds, Aitken was selected for the full Gala XV and, since that far-off day, he has never been dropped. A proud boast to be able to make in a club of such waxing forward strength over the past decade and a half.

His first two winters were spent mostly on the tight-head but, once Bob Cunningham had been translated from the second row to tight-head prop, Aitken moved across the front row to the berth in which he has won all his twenty-four caps.

He was barely 13½ stones in those days and along the way he was to have two horribly uncomfortable but salutary experiences which deepened his conviction that he had to add to his bulk, poundage and scrummaging strength. To wit, against Durham in his maiden game for the Scottish Border club, when the try he scored was scant consolation for a resounding defeat and his hapless evening against a gnarled North of England prop; and, in his first national trial, when he, Rodney Balfour and Struan McCallum, the latter two both very slimly built for their respective berths of hooker and tight-head prop, scrummaged against the celebrated triumvirate of Sandy Carmichael, Duncan Madsen and Ian McLauchlan.

Early in his days with Gala he had sought the advice of Ian McLauchlan. The Mighty Mouse had told how he himself had arrived at Jordanhill from Ayr Academy as an 11½-stone flanker but, by diligent but intelligent weight-training, built himself up to his eventual international weight of some 14½ stones. His international career over, McLauchlan has taken off that weight as readily as another might shed a suit of armour and it will be intriguing to see whether Aitken can do the same when his day is done. Be that as it may, the point is that he knew from the first precisely what he wanted to strengthen, his neck, back and legs, and he made sure that he was in the hands of the experts.

At Meadowbank he had the benefit not only of an international weight-lifter in Derek Gillies but of the company of such as Chris Black, Scotland's Olympic hammer-thrower, and Meg Ritchie, who won the women's discus in the Commonwealth Games. Meg Ritchie, in particular, had the knack of getting the best out of him 'because if a woman could do it . . .'

Aitken's collar size swelled from a mere 15 to 17½ but for a time he got carried away by his own enthusiasm and overdid it, going up to 16½ stones and finding that he could not get about the field as he wanted. One of that rare species who really enjoys his training – he likes to do something every day, even if it is only a lightish road run – the 5 ft 11 in Aitken has settled down at what he deems his best battling weight of 15 stones 8 lbs.

Three times capped at international B level, including a famous victory over the French at the Greenyards, Aitken first played for Scotland in the match against England at Twickenham in 1976 with Madsen and Carmichael his comrades in the front row. His immediate adversary was Fran Cotton, who was reputed to have found Aitken considerably less of a push-over, in more senses than one, than some had led him to envisage.

After three caps, Aitken gave way first to Ian McLauchlan, then to Jim Burnett and, finally, to McLauchlan again before he was brought back for the 1981 game with France at Parc de Princes. Significantly, it was Jim Telfer's first match as Scotland's coach.

He held his place right up until the historic defeat of Wales at Cardiff in 1982 when the try score was 5–1, the most improbable prelude, as Aitken says ruefully, to the imminent loss of his berth. So much has gone right for him in the interim that he looks back to the summer of 1982 and Scotland's tour of Australia with genuine incredulity rather than anything much in the way of bitterness. Yet, as he phrases it, he has still not been able to get to the bottom of why he was dropped in favour of Gerry McGuinness.

He had reckoned he was playing well. Possibly the explanation was no more sinister than that McGuinness had been tapping on the door for some time, particularly towards the end of the 1981 New Zealand tour, by which time his barrelled 17 stones had responded to the punishing training routines of that five-week tour.

The selectors may well have felt that McGuinness deserved his chance while Scotland had been hammered on the Saturday before the First Test by Sydney and, as football's Joe Mercer once wryly observed, it doesn't matter being old when the team are winning but when they lose that is the very thing you had best not be.

Passions run high in the Borders because, where rugby is concerned, they care so deeply and even within Gala circles Aitken has sometimes been a controversial figure.

Long moons ago he was sent off in a match against Selkirk at Philiphaugh. Arthur Brown missed a penalty attempt at goal and Aitken and an opponent tangled as Aitken came back from vain pursuit, the ball having been safely touched down for a drop-out.

He says himself that he was lucky in that not only was there a refereeing supervisor present but also a Scottish selector, not to mention Jock Wilson of the SRU and Robin Charters, then a selector for the South.

Charters gave evidence on his behalf and though the powers that be found that the referee, the erstwhile Esher hooker, Peter Wilmshurst, had been justified in the action he took, Aitken was cleared to play against Heriot's FP the very next day. The matter had been adjudicated upon on the Friday evening at what the SRU insisted was merely a previously arranged routine meeting of the disciplinary committee as opposed to one brought forward for Aitken's and Gala's convenience.

Those in the sporting limelight, especially nowadays, have to face their share of criticism, groundless or otherwise, and the tag that his detractors pinned on Aitken was that he was a trouble-maker who was yet reluctant to finish what he had started. But such voices faded as his international career mounted in the face of confrontation with such feared tight-heads as Paparemborde of France and Price of Wales while even his severest critics could not deny his triumphant record as pack leader and captain.

Aside altogether from his wonderful run with Scotland, he captained his adopted club, Gala, for four years in succession and twice to the Scottish title; a feat that has to be seen against the bizarre fact that that great club had only once previously emerged as Scottish champions and that as long ago as 1931–32. Last winter, he doubled up on captaining Scotland to a Grand Slam by doing the same thing with the South at inter-district level.

It was out in New Zealand with Scotland in 1981 that one got a real close-up of Aitken's powers of leadership as he led the side twice in Andy Irvine's absence, rekindling the fire doused by the defeat at Wellington. Often Jim Telfer would leave him in charge of the forwards while he and Irvine worked with the backs and one could not but be impressed, particularly by his influence on the scrummaging.

His approach, on his own submission, is by no means identical to that of Bill Dickinson, the former Scotland coach whose greatest renown lies in that department. Aitken believes that preconceived theories on the placement of the arms in binding and of the feet should often yield to the individual preference of a player. 'To me,' he constantly reiterates, 'by far the most important consideration is that each and every player in the scrum should be comfortable. As far as I'm concerned, the whole thing should be built around the hooker and what he wants because, after all, the first priority is to win your own ball and win it well.'

'You build from the front-row back and I should stress that in the Scotland pack the flankers are an absolutely vital part of our scrummage. Jim Calder is of inestimable value to me and David Leslie similarly knows exactly what Iain Milne likes. Our under-standing with our flankers in terms of the angle and height of the application of the shove is by now second nature to all involved.'

He does not think that the relatively recent strictures on binding have really eased the lot of the loose-head prop all that much and, indeed, he himself prefers to bind comparatively low rather than

Above Jim Aitken on the loose-head for Scotland with Colin Deans at hooker and Iain Milne on the tight-head. *George Herringshaw*

Below John Rutherford (left) and David Leslie exultantly bestow their congratulations on Jim Aitken for his try in Cardiff. *Bob Thomas*

high. That is partly because he likes to turn his opposite number inwards unless he is a prop in the mould of Iain Milne who, given half a chance, can come in on the enemy hooker and make his life a misery. In that instance, Aitken will drive as hard as he can on the tight-head's outside shoulder while bearing in mind the danger of getting too far away from his own hooker and splitting.

Seldom if ever can anyone say for sure who caused a scrum to collapse. Like many another loose-head, Aitken has been accused of taking the scrum down when in difficulties in the knowledge that the opposing tight-head is more likely to get the blame. Since such matters are apt to remain, like beauty, in the eye of the beholder, suffice to say that Aitken is well aware of the dangers of a collapsed scrum and, as the father of a twelve-year-old hooker, considers that England have got hold of a very good idea in their experimental law at schools level wherein a prop has to shove with his shoulders no lower than his hips.

'At international level and in first-class rugby as a whole,' he says, reflectively, 'the players are so hard, fit and experienced, they usually know intuitively how to come down in a collapsed scrum so as to escape injury. The snag with that law about scrummaging with the shoulders no lower than the hips is that it would negate much of the traditional craft of the Front Row Union. You could perhaps have a special law for schoolboys but I agree that the great worry would still lie in the area of the lower fifteens in a club and in so-called Coarse Rugby with the inexpert and unfit endeavouring to ape what they take to be the scrummaging tactics and antics of the international arena.'

He maintains that the degree to which the other countries in this year's International Championship were in a state of transition has tended to be exaggerated both inside and outside the media but willingly concedes that 'We were lucky to get Wales so early in the season and we caught Ireland on the hop.'

Not so long ago, Derek White, the Gala and Scotland forward, got married and it was said – though the full-back denies it – that when Andy Irvine was told that White had not asked any of the Gala backs to his wedding, he had quipped, 'Well, of course not, he wouldn't know them!' Apocryphal or not, it caught the image of a Gala XV who have relied heavily on their splendid forwards though, actually, when I have seen them, they have more than once played some very good football behind the scrum.

Aitken sees nothing wrong in a side playing to their strengths and says of Scotland in 1984 that 'We had limitations but we had the confidence of knowing that we could do what we did very well.

It showed in the tremendous defence when France had us under siege in the first half and it showed in our various moves in that we weren't just trying and hoping, but really expected them to come off, taking it damned near for granted.'

A good enough basketball player in his schooldays to have reached the Scottish area trials – his handling is ahead of many another international prop – Aitken has been asked countless times what he believes he has that sundry other captains lack. 'It is an impossible thing for me to answer without sounding either falsely modest or unbearably smug,' he shrugs. 'I do think, though, that I have two things going for me that some others don't.'

'In the first place, I definitely like to be in charge, as pack leader if I can't be captain. Secondly, I do so enjoy leading and/or captaining that, far from affecting my game adversely, as it arguably does that of such a great player as David Leslie, it really helps me to get going, to concentrate.'

There is, though he can hardly point to it himself, both a fibre and a competitiveness in the man which have manifested themselves revealingly even away from the rugby field. The son of a regimental sergeant-major in the Royal Scots, Aitken left school at the age of fifteen but ten years of night school and day release classes enabled him not only to take O and A levels but to finish up with both a diploma in Business Studies and a diploma in Industrial Engineering.

For the last nine years, he has been Managing Director of a firm of grain merchants and, typically, he has still found time to coach the team at George Watson's College for which his son, Russell, hooks. His younger son, the ten-year-old Neil, has as yet had only limited opportunities with a rugby ball but has taken so readily to golf as to suggest the aptitude of the natural games player. As for his wife, she is a veterinary surgeon and PhD. Nowadays, she is employed as a consultant in the delicate sphere of applying to human beings the benefit of drugs initially tried out upon animals having, in her days as a student, been the first woman ever to win the gold medal for her year.

'Gala down the years frequently had better players than the results suggested,' notes Jim Telfer. 'Jim Aitken's achievement has been to ensure that the sum of the whole was more worthy of the individual parts.' Of his successor as Scotland's captain, Andy Irvine says, 'He has a much more intelligent tactical appraisal than many are inclined to associate with prop forwards for all such precedents as Wilson Whineray. And, my word, when the ball is in his court, and circumstances call for half-backs kicking in support of a driving pack, he is in his element, capable of giving the operation a relentless force and cohesion.'

Aitken lost his record as an undefeated captain of Scotland in internationals when Scotland succumbed to Rumania in the broiling heat of Bucharest but he has no regrets at not having got out after the French match with his streak intact: 'That label had got out of all proportion and I am probably better without it.'

10
Beyond the Slam

'I don't know about a spin-off from the Grand Slam,' said David Leslie, dryly, some weeks after the victory over France, 'but the rip-off is going splendidly!'

Among the assorted opportunists springing to cash in on Triple Crown and Grand Slam with a miscellany of souvenirs were assuredly some who had long had the good of Scottish rugby at heart but there were plenty of others who would barely have known a scrum tunnel from the Mersey or Dartford.

The Grand Slam side were fêted at a variety of functions. That was as it should be and mostly they were much enjoyed, even if none quite produced a moment to rival that of the SRU's centenary celebrations when, at a reception in Edinburgh Castle, Alex Brown, a past Scotland stand-off and president of the SRU in 1971–72, hove to opposite a somewhat pompous military personage with an array of medals which Idi Amin would have considered ostentatious. 'I see,' nodded Alex, sympathetically, to the delight of those much more familiar with the sevens game than the nonplussed man-of-war, 'that you haven't got a Melrose one.'

The impact of the Grand Slam seemed at times of almost nuclear proportions but the conundrum was how to take this tide at the flood without ending up becalmed in a sea of complacency.

From several encouraging signs, one would content oneself with selecting just one: the fact that one-hundred-and-thirty schoolmasters attended an SRU national coaching course in August staged expressly for their benefit and run by Jim Telfer and the SRU's technical adviser, John Roxburgh. Just a year previously, the response had been so poor, a mere twenty-three, that the course had had to be cancelled.

The SRU nowadays tend to sell themselves much better than was the case when, some years ago, they appointed a public relations officer – John Law, who was already the secretary – but, by way of a first step in the new deal, omitted to tell anyone. It was no longer ago than 1972 either that, after the *Scotsman* newspaper had revealed that morning that the Ireland match in Dublin had been cancelled, the SRU gave birth to an official statement which was in its own way their *pièce de résistance*: that the match was 'neither on nor off'.

However, they have got a great deal more adept in the matter of handling the media, a turning point undoubtedly being Wilson Shaw's year as president for, as he said of the SRU's relationship with the media in general and the press in particular, 'We have been afraid for a very long time of something we have really no need to fear.'

The traditional image of the SRU was the reverse of avante garde and Alf Wilson, president in 1972–73, once expressed their attitude to change succinctly and only half tongue-in-cheek: 'We always say "No" – and then think about it.'

Besides leading the way with their installation of an electric blanket at Murrayfield and – in visiting South Africa in 1960 – pioneering the short tour, the SRU have shown a willingness to move with the times that no one could have visualized back in the blacker days of the Fifties, although they did introduce the Inter-District Championship in the first half of that decade.

They came to see that sponsorship was inevitable and that it had best be obtained while they were still in a position to ensure that it was on their terms. As to the advertising around the ground at Murrayfield, which would understandably have been abhorrent to bygone generations, they very properly revealed an eye for the main chance. In truth, I can remember sitting in the lounge of the Angel Hotel in Cardiff when a small SRU delegation who had gone to inspect the advertising at the Arms Park returned.

'How much did you say they were getting from it?' one of them asked.

'I gather,' I replied, 'it is something like £100,000 over a given span.'

'A £100,000?' breathed my interrogator, thoughtfully. 'You know it's really *very* tasteful.'

Their greatest achievement, in my eyes, aside from their recognition of the value of overseas tours in the evolution of the Scotland team, has been the way they organized the league structure once they bowed to the inevitable and saw that it was the will of the clubs. It is still not ideal and no one is more aware of that than the SRU but, considering the difficulties involved in the creation of such a structure, the job the championship committee did was worthy of the highest praise.

The attempt two years ago, by the SRU's Future of Scottish Rugby sub-committee, to introduce a calendar wherein the league rugby would be all over before the start of the Inter-District Championship, and the Inter-District Championship all over before the International Championship and a newly-inaugurated Scottish Cup, was altogether too much too soon. At the 1984 AGM, though the proposal by the sub-committee for First, Second and Third Divisions each comprising eight clubs and playing home and away fixtures, and five further Divisions each of fourteen clubs with single fixtures, failed to secure the necessary two-thirds majority, some thought from the show of hands that the vote was not too hopelessly removed from fifty-fifty.

The change from the original twelve-club leagues to fourteen-club leagues was, of course, inane as has been reflected in some of the astronomical scores recorded in the First Division. The First Division should certainly be reduced, and an eight-club division is regarded by most reformers as not too extreme. If that came to pass there would be reason for restoring the twelve-club leagues for the other Divisions if only because that would leave a little

The painting commemorating the 1984 Grand Slam by Ronnie Browne which was commissioned by The Royal Bank who sponsored Scotland's home internationals. Scottish rugby is also indebted to The Royal Bank for their sponsorship of the S R U Youth Leagues.

more room in terms of spare Saturdays for the first two rounds of a Scottish Cup, the advent of which remains a distinct possibility even if not in the immediate future.

Before the coming of the leagues the perennial weakness of Scottish rugby was too many clubs chasing too little talent. Sure enough, the leagues brought a greater concentration of better players though plainly not as great as it would be with an eight-club Premier League.

At present, many matches for the strongest clubs are undeniably too one-sided to have any great meaning but, in any reconstruction which takes place, particularly one involving the introduction of a Scottish Cup, authority must tread warily lest Scottish rugby go from one extreme to the other. The last thing one would want would be for the players to have such a diet of unrelenting pressure rugby that they ended up as drained for the international arena as many aver England's footballers are from their exacting League, League Cup and FA Cup programmes.

One other point may be made in passing. The Border spring and autumn sevens circuits, which mean so much to the Border clubs, not least financially, always take a lot of stick as a stumbling block to progress. However, with eleven Borderers in the Scotland XV which took the Triple Crown and Grand Slam, the time-honoured contention that so many sevens tournaments harm the standard of rugby has maybe sprung something of a leak.

There is now in Scotland a district and international framework at Under-15, Under-18, Under-19 and Under-21 levels with Youth rugby catering for those who leave school early and might otherwise drift out of the game. The Scottish Schools Cup got away to a remarkably encouraging start in 1983–84 even though the schools belonging to the Headmasters' Conference did not take part and there was no commercial sponsor.

The great worry at schools' level is that, though there are still many doing wonderful work far beyond the call of duty, there are fewer masters willing to help with rugby. Even in some schools with a proud rugby history there are real fears for the future while in others the amount of rugby material coming through has been unavoidably diluted by the decision to go co-educational.

In such sports as golf and rugby, the younger players are sifted so that the more promising may receive specialized coaching and, in the light of some of the changing trends in the schools and the problems they bring for rugby in their train, one especially welcomes the Player Improvement schemes which the SRU are increasingly keen to foster in the districts. They represent a sensible

Above left Freddie McLeod, convener of the S R U's Future of Scottish Rugby sub-committee and of the S R U's Schools Liaison sub-committee, in his playing days for Stewart's F P clearing against Hartlepool Rovers. *Glasgow Herald*

Above right Robin Young, the Biggar and Scotland Under-18 scrum-half, about to serve his stand-off in the match with West Germany, a fixture reflecting the changing horizons of modern rugby. *Dave Stranock*

Below Gary Parker, the Galashiels Academy and Scottish Schools scrum-half, in quest of a break versus Zimbabwe. Like David Johnston before Parker is currently playing football with Heart of Midlothian. *Dave Stranock*

recognition of an altered world wherein the schoolmasters, who once were out with their teams on a Saturday morning when most of their friends were still cooped up in offices, now know that, in this age of the five-day week, long before no-side, those same chums will be on about the ninth tee. The marvel is not that so many have defected but that so many have remained loyal to the cause.

The admirable reluctance of the SRU to rest on their oars is reflected in the calibre of the SRU's Future of Scottish Rugby sub-committee. The convener is the progressive and approachable Freddie McLeod, an all-rounder with a real feel for sport who was for thirteen seasons full-back for Stewart's FP. The others are the present convener of the Scottish selection committee, Robin Charters, and his two immediate predecessors, Ian MacGregor and Tom Pearson, together with Gordon Masson, the old Gordonians and North and Midlands scrum-half, and the former London Scottish and Scotland prop forward Cameron Boyle.

MacGregor and Pearson are both schoolmasters and fully cognisant of what is happening at that level while Freddie McLeod doubles as convener of the SRU's Schools Liaison sub-committee and the SRU's Future of Scottish Rugby sub-committee. They have all been in the forefront of the game at a time when, thanks in no small degree to television, Rugby Union has impinged on the public consciousness as never before; when major rugby internationals at Murrayfield have had to become all-ticket; and when, with greater media coverage, the greatest personalities in Scottish rugby have become household names in a manner which once was the preserve of the footballing fraternity.

By the same token, the men of the Future of Scottish Rugby sub-committee are wise enough to remember that rugby is only part of life, not life itself, for all that it may often seem so in the thrilling maelstrom of an international. They are the more likely to have the right perspective in never forgetting that there is a world elsewhere. A fact never more perfectly illustrated than in that story, which bears repetition, of the day Andy Irvine, in kicking a goal against Hawick at Goldenacre, put the ball through the window of one of the neighbouring houses. Some small Heriot's schoolboys were sent to retrieve it and, ringing the doorbell, asked the lady who answered if they could please have the ball back.

'Who did it?' screamed the woman, furiously.

'Please Miss, it was Andy Irvine.'

'And which one of you,' stormed the woman, 'is Andy Irvine?'

11
The First Immortals

In 1925 it was not just the cricketers who had their Wisden *but also the rugby players and the extracts from that Almanack which follow convey the contemporary feel of that great year. Five of Scotland's first Grand Slam team lived to see the second Grand Slam: Dan Drysdale, Herbert Waddell, Bob Howie, Jimmy Ireland and Doug Davies. Ireland, who knew that 1925 side from the depths of the scrum as the hooker, and Drysdale, who had the full-back's panoramic view, look back (at the end of this chapter) across the decades to that vintage season.*

THE INTERNATIONAL CHAMPIONSHIP

Winning all their four matches, Scotland carried off the International Championship. They had narrowly missed that honour two years previously, when only a wonderful place-kick led to their defeat by England, and in 1920 they shared first honours with England and Wales, but eighteen years had elapsed since they last proved successful in all their Championship matches, and in those days France did not figure in the competition. Their triumph last season was thoroughly deserved. They opened with brilliant victories over France and Wales, followed with a hard-earned win against Ireland at Dublin, and wound up with a desperately close struggle with England on the new ground at Murrayfield, where success attended their efforts by fourteen points to eleven. The victory over England, although restricted to a matter of three points, furnished matter for special rejoicing in Scottish football circles in view of the fact that the seven immediately preceding contests between the two countries had all resulted in the defeat of the northern kingdom. For England, who had not sustained a single reverse in the International Championship competition since the match at Cardiff in the early days of 1922, the season naturally proved rather disappointing, but certainly no one could grudge the Scotsmen their long delayed triumph. As it was, England, if never the convincing side they had been in the two previous years, cut by no means a poor figure, seeing that they overcame Wales and France, drew with Ireland and gave Scotland so hard a game. Ireland, after the fine fight made with the New Zealanders, were strongly fancied in many quarters for the championship, and they probably commanded the strongest defence of any of the five countries. Although beating France in Paris, they did not produce their best form on that occasion, but they might well, on the play at Twickenham, have overcome England, and they defeated Wales in handsome fashion, but before this success against the Principality they had ruined their chances of first honours by losing to Scotland at Dublin. Still, if the highest distinction eluded their grasp, the Irishmen gave a better account of themselves than in any season since the war. For the second year in succession Wales only escaped the 'wooden spoon' by a victory over France. Their forwards worked hard and the team that took the field at Twickenham looked to possess distinct possibilities, but radical changes in the back division for the remaining contests led to disastrous results and a narrow defeat from England was followed by heavy reverses inflicted by Scotland and Ireland. France made a hard fight with Ireland, a still better one with England, and were by no means outplayed by Wales, even if they went down badly before Scotland. And yet, with defeat their portion in all four games, they had a worse record than in any of the five preceding seasons.

SCOTLAND (25) v FRANCE (4)

Played at Inverleith, 24 January 1925

Scotland began their most successful season since the war with a substantial victory at the expense of the Frenchmen, scoring two goals and five tries (25 points) to a dropped goal (4 points). This engagement also saw the end of the Inverleith enclosure as a venue for international matches in the Scottish capital. The needs of modern rugby had outgrown its capacity and in March a move was made to Murrayfield. Scotland took leave of their old home with a win (they had opened it with a defeat) and entered into possession of their splendid new enclosure in a blaze of triumph which gave them the International Championship.

If in the game with France the Scottish forwards scarcely attained to the standard that subsequently characterized their work, their backs were splendid. In J. B. Nelson was found a worthy successor to Bryce, and J. C. Dykes, coming in for Waddell, rose to the occasion well. At all points of the scrum-half game Nelson showed international form. He got the ball out quickly: at other times he cut through with a powerful hand-off, and his defence proved almost invariably sound. Thus there existed in a special degree the important source from which the three-quarter line – composed entirely of Oxford University players – found means to exploit their combination to the best advantage. Aitken did not get off the mark well, though playing better the longer the game lasted, and a damaged wrist caused some inconvenience to Wallace, but the other two – Macpherson and Smith – were brilliant. Wallace ran finely and made full use of his chances, showing class in all that he did. To Smith, however, the game brought the greatest distinction. Admitting that he had some glorious openings made for him – his partner drawing the defence most skilfully – Smith showed that he had profited by his South African trip. He ran with the greatest determination, some of his dashes for the line being magnificent. The value of speed and straight running was in his case eloquently emphasized for of the seven tries Scotland obtained he could claim no fewer than four. Drysdale gave everyone anxiety by the way he began, but happily for Scotland a fit of poor handling and bad kicking soon passed, and long before the end he was himself once more.

Forward Scotland scarcely gave satisfaction. It may sound a little ungenerous to criticize the pack when victory came so readily, but there was an absence of cohesion among them. Gillies, Buchanan, Bannerman and Scott did well and yet, generally speaking, the forwards missed being great. They lacked that wonderful dash that is such a pronounced feature of Scottish forward play. Badly led they never got really together.

Nothing in the trial matches had suggested that the French team were likely to cause much trouble, and the sequel proved that these surmises were correct. The visitors gave a disappointing exhibition especially behind the scrummage. They could not complain of lack of opportunity, the forwards doing quite a lot of smart heeling, but the three-quarters parted with the ball long before they had reached their opposite number and thus Scotland generally had a man extra in defence. With the game going steadily against them in the second half, the Frenchmen took a new lease of life and did a lot of hard pressing, yet few of their attacks looked like being successful. A little more dash near the line was sadly wanted. Du Manoir, the stand-off half, on his first appearance in the United Kingdom, gave a great display. Unconventional for a French player, he often went through unassisted and his left-foot dropped goal was a sparkling achievement. Ducousso, too, at full-back, proved himself a fine tackler.

Over twenty thousand people saw the match. In about five minutes Scotland took the lead, Gillies going over and, with a clever kick, converting the try himself. For the most part the play during the early stages was with the forwards. Twice the Frenchmen broke away and in one attack Du Manoir, from well beyond the twenty-five yards line, dropped a glorious goal, the ball sailing well between the line of and high above the posts. Scotland had the best of matters but did not add to their one point lead before half-time.

Change of ends saw a different Scotland who, touching their best form, put on 14 points in the next eighteen minutes. Wallace and Smith each scored two tries and Drysdale placed a goal. There followed a period of pronounced pressure by France, but the Scottish defence held up and then Scotland, taking charge of the game once more, finished up in brilliant fashion. Smith, with tremendous bursts of speed, crossed France's line twice more and three minutes after the last try the game ended.

SCOTLAND D. Drysdale (Heriotonians); A. C. Wallace (Oxford University), G. G. Aitken (Oxford University), G. P. S. Macpherson (Oxford University), I. S. Smith (Oxford University); J. C. Dykes (Glasgow Academicals), J. B. Nelson (Glasgow Academicals); J. M. Bannerman (Glasgow High School FP), J. C. R. Buchanan (Stewartonians), J. Gilchrist (Glasgow Academicals), A. C. Gillies (Watsonians), D. J. MacMyn (Cambridge University), J. R. Paterson (Birkenhead Park), J. W. Scott (Stewartonians), W. H. Stevenson (Glasgow Academicals).

FRANCE J. Ducousso (Stade Tarbais); L. Raymond (Stade Toulousain), J. Ballarin (Stade Tarbais), J. Baillette (US Perpignan), J. Halet (AS Strasbourg); Y. Du Manoir (Racing Club de France), C. Dupont (FC de Lourdes); A. Maury (State Toulousain), A. Montade (US Perpignan), C. Marcet (SC Albi), F. Laurent (Biarritz Olympique), A. Cassayet (RC Narbonnais), A. Boubee (Biarritz Olympique), A. Ribère (US Perpignan), L. Bioussa (Stade Toulousain).

Referee Dr E. De Courcy Wheeler (Ireland).

WALES (14) v SCOTLAND (24)

Played at Swansea, 7 February 1925

A victory by a placed goal, a dropped goal and five tries to a placed goal, a penalty goal and two tries – 24 points to 14 – rewarded the efforts of the Scotsmen in this, their second international match of the season. Brilliant indeed was the form of Scotland up to half-time, and for a little time afterwards. Everything pointed to Wales being defeated as thoroughly as in the corresponding engagement at Edinburgh the previous year, but in this respect expectations were far from being realized, for the Scotsmen lost their form in a most unaccountable manner, and, if in no great danger of being beaten, had much of their substantial lead taken from them. It is quite likely that Scotland, finding themselves so far in front, took matters a little light-heartedly, and, when they wanted to reproduce their previous astonishing work, could not rise to the occasion. Their forwards 'cracked' and the Welsh pack, quick to discover the falling-off, made a gallant attempt to pull the game out of the fire. The great rally of the Welshmen in the second half did much to retrieve a sadly-tarnished reputation, and, at the same time, the failure of the Scottish forwards to last created a feeling of uncertainty as to their exact value which was not entirely dispelled until they gained their triumph in the match with England.

Beyond all question the form of the Scottish Fifteen at every point reached its highest during the first half of the game at Swansea. In no other match did the side reveal such wonderful powers in attack. Quick in settling down, the forwards not only scrummaged splendidly, but broke up so smartly that they brushed the opposition out of the way before the Welshmen realized what had happened. With their forwards dominating the scrummages and outplaying their opponents in the loose, the Scottish backs, rarely called upon for big efforts in defence, were able to develop their attacks in a manner possible only to men with a complete understanding of each other. On the occasions when the pack did not go through with the ball, they heeled well and, Nelson and Dykes being in good form at half, the ball was often with the three-quarters. Admirably did these men carry out their part of the work, handling beautifully and running with rare determination and skill.

Ignoring for the moment their faulty play of the second half, it may be said that the key-note of the game was struck in the first minute when the ball went right across the three-quarter line, a gloriously ordered movement ending in Smith racing right away to beat Johnson and score in an easy position for Drysdale to place a goal. There were many other attacks of a similar character, some of them successful, the play generally giving the impression that here was a tip-top International Fifteen engaged in a match with a very ordinary club side. Pace, above everything else, was with the Scotsmen, and Wales, although they worked hard – especially Delahay at scrum-half – were quite incapable of coping with the dazzling play of their opponents.

Nothing was better than the strong finishing of Smith and Wallace, the wing-threequarters. Certainly they owed much to the clever play of their inside men, Macpherson in particular making some beautiful openings for his partner on the left, but all the same Scotland would scarcely have done so well had not Smith and Wallace – each with a fine sense of anticipation – been in their positions ready to take a pass and complete a movement success-fully. Giving every credit to the forwards, among whom Gillies, Davies, Bannerman, Ireland and MacMyn were always prominent, it was the three-quarters who won the match for Scotland by running up such a big score before the forwards let the side down in the last twenty minutes of the match. So far as actual scoring was concerned, Smith, as in the game with France, proved the hero. Following his first try he put on two others by the time the game was a quarter of an hour old, the first of these being made possible by Macpherson, who cleared the way with a very clever dummy. From just outside the twenty-five yards line, Drysdale, who later on was to accomplish great things in defence, dropped a fine goal and before half-time Wales's discomfiture was completed with a try by Wallace, who, getting well into his stride, twice handed off Johnson. Leading by eighteen points to none at half-time, Scotland went further ahead when Wallace scored another try less than five minutes after the resumption, and although Hopkins got over for Wales for Parker to place a goal, this did not stop the Scotsmen, Smith, with a great individual run, scoring his fourth try of the match.

Then it was that the tide turned. From being a great pack the Scotsmen deteriorated sadly. They lost their shoving power, pace and cleverness, and for the rest of the time were disorganized. Fortunately for them, the Scottish backs were almost as good in defence as they had been in attack, but they could not prevent the Welshmen from crossing their line twice more, Idris Jones going over in a forward rush and Cornish picking up in some loose play

Above 7 February 1925: Scotland 24 Wales 14. The players (left to right):
back row G. G. Aitken, J. C. H. Ireland, D. J. MacMyn, J. W. Scott,
D. J. Davies, R. A. Howie, I. S. Smith;
middle row A. C. Gillies, J. M. Bannerman, G. P. S. Macpherson (capt),
D. Drysdale, A. C. Wallace, J. R. Paterson;
front row J. B. G. Nelson, J. C. Dykes.
Below A. C. Wallace scoring one of Scotland's six tries at St Helen's.
BBC Hulton Picture Library

to get the last try of the game. Parker subsequently kicked a penalty goal, and on another occasion failed from a fairly easy position.

The strong finish made by the Welshmen saved the match from being a rout, but, giving Wales every credit for this, they were not a good side. No form at all was shown by the Welsh backs until their forwards stopped the rushes of the Scottish pack, and above everything else they lacked pace.

WALES T. Johnson (Cardiff); W. James (Aberavon), R. A. Cornish (Cardiff), Evan Williams (Aberavon), C. Thomas (Bridgend); W. J. Hopkins (Aberavon), W. J. Delahay (Cardiff); C. Pugh (Maesteg), S. Morris (Cross Keys), Bryn Phillips (Aberavon), S. Herrara (Cross Keys), W. Idris Jones (Llanelli and Cambridge University), D. Parker (Swansea), Idris Richards (Cardiff), S. Lawrence (Bridgend).

SCOTLAND D. Drysdale (Heriotonians); A. C. Wallace (Oxford University), G. G. Aitken (Oxford University), G. P. S. Macpherson (Oxford University), I. S. Smith (Oxford University); J. C. Dykes (Glasgow Academicals), J. B. Nelson (Glasgow Academicals); J. M. Bannerman (Glasgow High School FP), D. S. Davies (Hawick), A. C. Gillies (Watsonians), R. Howie (Kirkcaldy), J. C. H. Ireland (Glasgow High School FP), J. R. Paterson (Birkenhead Park), D. J. MacMyn (Cambridge University), J. W. Scott (Stewartonians).

Referee J. W. Baxter (England).

IRELAND (8) v SCOTLAND (14)
Played at Dublin, 28 February 1925

Earlier matches in which the countries had taken part clearly suggested that upon the result of the meeting of Ireland and Scotland might depend the International Championship. Scotland won – scoring two placed goals and a dropped goal to a placed goal and a penalty goal, or fourteen points to eight – and they went on to overcome England, but before they got through with Ireland they had many anxious moments in a game brimful of excitement from start to finish. Indeed with about six minutes remaining for play they led by only two points, and anything might have happened. With the issue thus hanging in the balance Waddell dropped a goal for Scotland – just as he subsequently did against

England – to decide the result. Ireland made one final effort but the Scottish defence held out.

For this victory Scotland had, without any question at all, to thank their forwards. If not so brilliant in their execution as in the first half against Wales, they played consistently well from start to finish, and, so far from going to pieces as their doings at Swansea suggested they might, they lasted out a tremendously hard struggle in really wonderful fashion. As to how the game would have gone if Macpherson had been available – he was injured in the Welsh match – opinions may be divided. Possibly Scotland would have triumphed readily, for Dykes, who had played at stand-off half in the previous engagement, scarcely rose to the occasion when brought in as a substitute for the Scottish captain in the three-quarter line. He did not actually fail, but his partner, Smith, found the opportunities of using his pace restricted, and when he did get away the close marking of Harry Stephenson prevented him from being that dominating power in attack of which both France and Wales had had such devastating proof. Of the two three-quarter lines Scotland certainly looked, and actually were, the more danger-ous, Wallace being the outstanding player of the eight. The Scots-men ran straight and strongly, whereas the Irish three-quarters, as in the first half against England at Twickenham, went across the field too much to bore their wing men on to the touch line. Wallace was in a class by himself. In attack a constant source of danger with his fine running and clever side-stepping, he, by great tackling, held up the Irish left-wing time after time. For most of the second half his task in this respect was a comparatively light one, T. Hewitt going very lame and, although continuing very pluckily, being of little further use to his side. Kept out of the earlier games through injuries, Waddell returned to his accustomed position at stand-off half and made his presence felt at once. Excellent in defence when Ireland were carrying the scrums he came into his own in attack directly the Scottish forwards began to get possession, and in most of the passing movements by Scotland one could trace in him the master mind. He combined admirably with Nelson.

Nothing in the match was better than the doings of the full-backs. Crawford, for Ireland, played probably as well as ever he had, but his work paled before that of Drysdale, who did not make a single mistake. Whether tackling, fielding the ball, or kicking, Drysdale proved not only thoroughly dependable but at times positively brilliant. In this match he touched the highest form of his career.

Both individually and collectively the Scottish forwards will always be able to look back upon their performance against Ireland in 1925 with the utmost degree of satisfaction. At the outset they certainly were beaten for possession, but, once they had settled down, they became a great pack, and, just as the Irishmen had had the best of the struggle with England, the Scottish forwards similarly exercised a superiority over those of Ireland. Severe as it was the loss of Gillies did not greatly upset them. They got down to the scrums quickly, broke up well, maintained a splendid pace, and at no time showed any suspicion of falling off. All did well but nobody better than MacMyn, who throughout the game was to the fore in everything. For Ireland, Clinch, Browne and Beamish came through the match quite well, but in the whole of the pack there was a lack of finishing power which probably made the difference between winning and losing.

There had been a lot of heavy rain during the week, but happily the game took place in very pleasant weather. Still the turf was distinctly on the soft side, and when play had been in progress some little time the ball became greasy and rather difficult to handle with accuracy. Ireland began with strong pressure, T. Hewitt being held up close to the line, and although Scotland cleared they had for a long time to meet several strong attacks. In this work Drysdale, although helped rather by the Irish forwards kicking too hard in their rushes, was admirable and, as much as anybody else, was responsible for keeping the Irishmen out, his touch finding being a model of accuracy and length. Not until five minutes before half-time did Scotland take the lead. They had steadily driven the Irishmen back and Aitken got away and tried to cut through. He realized that further progress was impossible so he passed out and the ball reaching Wallace quickly that player was able to dart over the line with scarcely anyone to trouble him. Drysdale converted with a fine kick.

Once more Ireland opened with powerful attacks, but their forwards soon began to feel the effects of the great pace and were not so quick in getting down to the scrums. In turn Ireland had to defend stoutly, but they reduced Scotland's lead when from a long way out Crawford, with a magnificent kick, landed a penalty goal. Just before this T. Hewitt had been injured and with Browne pulled out of the pack to take his place Ireland were handicapped a good deal. The Scottish backs brought off a number of good passing movements and ultimately MacMyn went over with a try after Wallace, Aitken, Dykes and Scott had handled. Dykes placed a goal and Scotland led by ten points to three, but directly afterwards Harry Stephenson scored for Ireland for Crawford to place a goal from near the touch line. There was some discussion afterwards about this try, for Stephenson, who was well up to the ball when it went into touch, threw it into play and catching it himself ran in near the corner, the score being quite legitimate but somewhat unusual. Only two points separating the scores the finish of the match was full of excitement, but Waddell clinched matters by dropping a goal when the Irishmen expected him to pass and a little later the game ended with Ireland attacking.

IRELAND W. E. Crawford (Lansdowne); H. W. V. Stephenson (United Services), G. V. Stephenson (Queen's University, Belfast), J. B. Gardiner (North of Ireland), T. Hewitt (Queen's University, Belfast); F. S. Hewitt (Instonians), M. Sugden (Dublin University); G. R. Beamish (Coleraine and RAF), W. F. Browne (United Services), J. D. Clinch (Dublin University), W. R. F. Collis (Wanderers), R. Collopy (Bective Rangers), R. Y. Crichton (Dublin University), J. C. McVicker (Belfast Collegians), M. J. Bradley (Dolphin).

SCOTLAND D. Drysdale (Heriotonians); A. C. Wallace (Oxford University), G. G. Aitken (Oxford University), J. C. Dykes (Glasgow Academicals), I. S. Smith (Oxford University); H. Waddell (Glasgow Academicals), J. B. Nelson (Glasgow Academicals); J. M. Bannerman (Glasgow High School FP), J. C. R. Buchanan (Stewartonians), D. S. Davies (Hawick), R. Howie (Kirkcaldy), J. C. H. Ireland (Glasgow High School FP), D. J. MacMyn (Cambridge University), J. W. Scott (Stewartonians), J. R. Paterson (Birkenhead Park).

Referee A. E. Freethy (Wales).

SCOTLAND (14) v ENGLAND (11)
Played at Murrayfield, 21 March 1925

One can say without exaggeration that the match between Scotland and England on the new ground of the Scottish Rugby Union will live long in the memory of those privileged to be present. There was not a dull moment from start to finish, the wealth of incident crowded into the eighty minutes over which the game extended being quite remarkable. In its pace, skill and varying fortunes this historic struggle provided a fitting climax to a splendid season's rugby. Scotland won, a dropped goal in the closing stages changing the lead for the third time and deciding the issue. With their victory by 14 points to 11 (represented by two placed goals and a dropped goal to a placed goal, a penalty goal and a try), the Scottish Fifteen carried off the International Championship and also the Calcutta Cup, of which England had held uninterrupted possession since 1913. Incidentally this was only the second success registered by the representatives of the Northern Kingdom against England in eleven matches.

Leaving aside for the moment the play and its result the match had special claims for remembrance. It marked a fresh era in the history of Scottish rugby, taking place, as it did, in such circumstances. Inverleith, the former headquarters of the game in Scotland, had ever since the war been recognized as scarcely adequate for the requirements of modern international encounters. Consequently a move was made to Murrayfield, on the western side of the city, where, at enormous expense, and in a remarkably short space of time, had been provided a truly magnificent venue. Never before in the history of the game, in the United Kingdom at any rate, has a rugby international match taken place amid a nobler setting. The doings of the Scottish Fifteen in their earlier struggles aroused the greatest possible interest, and with the championship depending upon the result – Scotland had only to draw to make themselves certain of that honour – a record attendance was assured. People came from all parts, and while the official figures have not been given out by the Scottish Union, there must have been, at a rough estimate, close upon eighty thousand present. This, one scarcely need remark, is easily the largest company ever seen at a rugby match. Happily the inauguration of Murrayfield was especially favoured by the weather. The sun shone from almost a cloudless sky, with a pleasant breeze, never strong enough to interfere with the play, to keep the temperature within normal bounds.

Recovered from the damage which kept him out of the Irish match, Macpherson was able to take his place in the Scottish three-quarter line to captain the side, and, no defections occurring, Scotland had their best team. England, too, chose the strongest available Fifteen, neither G. S. Conway nor Leo Price having got over the injuries sustained earlier in the season. As it was the English pack, at any rate, showed their best form of the season even if not quite the equals of the opposing eight.

Paradoxical though it may sound Scotland were a little lucky to win, yet had they lost they would have been the victims of the grossest ill-fortune. They were that little the better in general tactics and pace to make the result quite just and equitable. It would be hard to speak in terms of too high praise of the wonderful work of Scotland's pack. Possessing in Ireland a really first-class hooker they heeled more smartly than their opponents and in the loose exercised a pronounced superiority, nothing in the whole match being finer than some of their rushes during the second half. Admirably led by Bannerman, Gillies, MacMyn and Scott, they swept down the field in relentless fashion with the ball beautifully under control and, even when sometimes checked, carried on the movement to gain further ground. In face of all this the English defence held up in remarkable manner. No one hesitated to go down to the ball, the tackling on both sides being tremendous. But for a couple of regrettable incidents – certain players lost their heads – which had perhaps better be forgotten at this distance of time, one could write much more enthusiastically of the English forwards. In their different ways Wakefield and Voyce touched a very high standard. Probably neither of them had ever played so well, while of the others Tucker, Luddington, and the two younger members of the pack, Maclennan and Cumming, acquitted themselves most creditably in the close work and in helping to stem those fierce onslaughts which will ever be an abiding memory.

Behind the scrummage Scotland were the more finished team, and what was of the greatest importance they possessed that extra pace which, when they had the ball, made them more formidable in attack. The ball coming out on their side of the scrummage so often as it did, Nelson and Waddell naturally had more chances than Massey and Myers, and admirably did they rise to the occasion. Nelson was particularly quick in getting the ball away, while Waddell, whether in attack or defence, demonstrated clearly that he was the best stand-off half of the season. Alert in seizing upon an opening, Waddell got his three-quarters moving with some splendid passes, while individually he was always a source of anxiety to the English defence. To him, as will be told later, belonged the distinction of dropping the goal which won the match, while his partner Nelson scored the try from which Drysdale kicked a goal to give Scotland the lead for the first time after Luddington's penalty goal for England.

The play going mostly on the other side of the field, or through the centre, not much was seen of Smith, but Wallace, Macpherson and Aitken all attained to great excellence, Macpherson and the two halves being the men whom England had most to fear among the backs. Perhaps Macpherson and Aitken were prone to overdo the cutting through, but as this form of attack came off successfully on one occasion, little complaint could be made. So far as their tackling was concerned, they were all splendid, bringing their man down time after time in no uncertain fashion. Drysdale, at full-back, did all that was asked of him, and certainly outshone Holliday, but one could not resist the conviction that the Englishmen played into his hands far too much.

Not much fault could be found with the way Massey came through the game, but Myers showed that he had seen his best days, for he kicked with unnecessary frequency and seemed for some reason or other to be afraid of trusting his three-quarters. As some excuse it is only proper to observe that he was very badly shaken up in the first half and one was told afterwards that until late in the game he did not actually know which way England were playing. Up to a point Locke did very well, but spoilt a lot of otherwise excellent work by doing the wrong thing after cutting out a beautiful opening. Corbett, too, was not by any means himself, but Hamilton-Wickes, if not favoured with many chances, came through a hard match in satisfactory style and enjoyed the distinction of getting nearly the best try of the game. Still as a line the English three-quarters did not possess the fire and pace of the other four. Form had pointed to Scotland winning and in running their opponents so close the English team accomplished perhaps rather more than had been expected of them. They went all out and some could scarcely limp off the field at the finish of one of the fastest matches ever seen.

The game opened with some attacks by Scotland, both sides being quickly in their stride, but in less than ten minutes England went in front. A smart interception by Locke followed by a run and a punt ahead carried play to the Scottish line, where Scotland being penalized, Luddington promptly kicked a goal. The forward play which followed was very good indeed, and although the Scottish pack seemed better together the Englishmen broke up quickly and often stopped the attempts of Nelson and Waddell to open the game. At the end of twenty-five minutes Scotland obtained the lead. Macpherson took a wide pass, and giving a beautiful 'dummy', slipped through the defence before handing the ball to Aitken. In turn Nelson got possession, and in a splendid burst of twenty yards he handed off Holliday in great style to score under the posts, Drysdale placing a goal. Encouraged by this success, Scotland then delivered a number of tremendous attacks, and in turn Nelson and Bannerman were almost in. As a set off to this, England brought off one glorious movement, the attack going first on the right and then on the left with seven men, among them

Hamilton-Wickes, Cumming, Wakefield, Locke and Myers, handling the ball. Near half-time England went ahead once more. Smith on the left misfielded an awkwardly bouncing ball, and in a flash Hamilton-Wickes dashed up and gained possession. Running a little distance he found Voyce in attendance and gave the Gloucester man a pass to carry on the movement. Facing Drysdale, Voyce returned the ball to Hamilton-Wickes, who scored a really brilliant try from which Luddington kicked a goal. England at the interval led by eight points to five, an advantage scarcely justified by the run of the play.

Within five minutes of the resumption England added to their score, Wakefield, following up well and dropping on to the ball as it went over the line from a cross-kick by Corbett. The kick at goal was from a very easy position, and nothing seemed more certain than that England would in a moment or two be leading by eight clear points. As the ball was being placed the Scottish forwards rushed out. Corbett at once lifted the ball up, the referee blew his whistle, and the Scottish forwards stopped. But as the ball was placed on the ground again, nearly everyone thinking the charge had been disallowed, the home forwards came on and kicked it away, to the obvious surprise of all the Englishmen. Whether this incident affected the ultimate result it is impossible to say, but there is no doubt that Mr Freethy, the referee – who otherwise did his work admirably – was quite in error in permitting the Scottish forwards to go on after blowing his whistle.

Ten minutes later, following some desperate attacks, Scotland scored again when Wallace got over. This point also caused some discussion, the corner flag being knocked down as Wallace ran in, but after consulting the touch judge the referee allowed the try. Gillies placing a goal with a very fine kick, only one point separated the scores, and as will readily be imagined, the rest of the game was fought out in an atmosphere of the most intense excitement. Playing a wonderful game, the Scottish forwards made attack after attack, being held up only by the most fearless tackling, and on one occasion Aitken, in trying to dribble over the line, kicked the ball against one of the uprights. As it rebounded, Waddell gained possession and went only just wide in an attempt to drop a goal. These were indeed two marvellous escapes. However, after Smith had been nearly over on the left, Waddell got the ball once more, and this time he dropped a beautiful goal. Scotland were now three points in front, the end being very near, but before 'no side' came they themselves had many anxious moments, for the Englishmen made almost superhuman efforts to get on terms. First Smallwood was nearly in on the left, and Locke made a brilliant cut through, but was overtaken, while, with the ball going towards the right, Corbett seemed certain to score. He had only a yard or two to go after a good run, but, at his last gasp, he did not possess the physical strength sufficient to hurl himself over the line, and was held up when it seemed at his mercy. Twice Myers tried to force his way over, and then, with Corbett just failing to drop a goal, a wonderful match came to an end.

SCOTLAND D. Drysdale (Heriotonians); A. C. Wallace (Oxford University), G. G. Aitken (Oxford University), G. P. S. Macpherson (Oxford University), I. S. Smith (Oxford University); H. Waddell (Glasgow Academicals), J. B. Nelson (Glasgow Academicals); J. M. Bannerman (Glasgow High School FP), J. C. H. Ireland (Glasgow High School FP), J. W. Scott (Stewartonians), D. S. Davies (Hawick), D. J. MacMyn (Cambridge University), R. H. Howie (Kirkcaldy), J. R. Paterson (Birkenhead Park), A. C. Gillies (Watsonians).

ENGLAND T. E. Holliday (Aspatria); R. H. Hamilton-Wickes (Harlequins), L. J. Corbett (Bristol), H. M. Locke (Birkenhead Park), A. M. Smallwood (Leicester); E. Myers (Bradford), E. J. Massey (Leicester); W. W. Wakefield (Harlequins), R. Cove-Smith (Old Merchant Taylors), A. F. Blakiston (Liverpool), J. S. Tucker (Bristol), W. G. E. Luddington (Devonport Services), R. R. F. Maclennan (Old Merchant Taylors), A. T. Voyce (Gloucester), D. C. Cumming (Cambridge University).

Referee A. E. Freethy (Wales).

SCOTLAND'S FINE TEAM

S. J. Southerton

Scottish International form touched its highest mark for many years in the season of 1924–5. All four matches were won and, for the first time since 1906–7, Scotland carried off the Championship outright, their nearest approach to this being in 1920 when they shared the honour with England and Wales. That they deserved their success in every way there could be no two opinions. In certain respects the team – which like all first-class sides underwent but few alterations from time to time – had their limitations. When, however, the crucial test – the match with England – came they did all that was necessary and, as is told elsewhere, rose to a great occasion in wonderful style. In their struggle with Wales, Scotland left the impression that they were non-stayers. Indeed, it was more than an impression. They actually demonstrated the process of 'cracking' in no uncertain fashion. Thus was created the belief that against England they would fail to last, more particularly if the weather was at all warm – conditions which more than once in former years had conduced to their undoing. Seldom have ideas on this point been more rudely shattered. The struggle for the Calcutta Cup was fought out on a bright spring afternoon with the sun shining, but Scotland, though hard pressed in the later stages, never broke and went to a victory that stamped the fifteen as worthy victors in the great annual tournament between the countries. The result of this particular game was, from the Scottish point of view, the more gratifying as it marked a new era in the history of rugby in the Northern Kingdom. After many seasons at Inverleith, the headquarters of the game was transferred to the magnificent new enclosure at Murrayfield.

Scotland began well against France, but to close judges of the game it was obvious that the forwards were not all they might have been. Proper leadership of the pack was lacking and no surprise came when three of them had to stand down from the Welsh match. Buchanan was one of these, and the other two – Gilchrist and Stevenson – failed to regain their places. Indeed, not until the game with England did the forwards become a really cohesive and well balanced body, able to shove, heel, and break away in the traditional Scottish style. Against Wales they played brilliantly in the first half only to go completely to pieces in the second. Scotland in this engagement had to thank the magnificent work of their backs for running up a score sufficiently large to enable them to pull through, although in the later stages the whole side was being outplayed.

Meanwhile D. S. Davies, R. A. Howie (old internationals) and J. C. H. Ireland had come into the pack and they were not afterwards disturbed, but Buchanan, with Gillies unable to play, found favour again for the Irish match only to be dropped for the encounter with England, by which time Gillies had recovered. Even against Ireland, Scotland, well as they played, were not quite convincing, as far as estimating what their chances would be with England. This, however, was not the fault of the forwards. J. C. Dykes who, with Waddell unfit, had partnered Nelson at half in the first two matches, was moved to the three-quarter line when Waddell found himself able to turn out, and appeared as inside to

Smith. Dykes acquitted himself well enough, but did not create the openings for the speedy winger that Macpherson had against France and Wales. An injury to the leg sustained at Swansea kept Macpherson out of the game at Dublin and the loss of this fine player upset the combination. Still all was well for the final encounter at Murrayfield when, as against Ireland, Waddell demonstrated his great value and Macpherson made the three-quarter line complete once more. In all Scotland called upon only 19 players for their four games. Drysdale, the full-back, Wallace, Aitken and Smith, the three-quarters, Nelson the scrum-half and Bannerman, MacMyn, Paterson and Scott of the forwards took part in every one; Macpherson, Dykes, Gillies, Davies, Howie and Ireland in three; Waddell and Buchanan in two; and Gilchrist and Stevenson in one each.

Although it took the greater part of the season for the pack to come into form, the backs were, from the very start, at their best and to this fact Scotland owed their championship success. In Drysdale they had the best full-back in the four countries. Against France he began badly enough, but recovered well and never afterwards looked back, his fielding, kicking and tackling being such as to stamp him of the highest class. Naturally with such a dependable player behind them the rest of the team could have had little or no anxiety. But it was the three-quarter line that made the side such a magnificent and telling force in attack. Oxford men all – three of them were in the successful Oxford fifteen and Smith played the previous year – they enjoyed the supreme advantage of knowing each other's play intimately. Wallace and Macpherson stood out as the brains of the line – the former by his individuality and Macpherson by the delightful manner in which he made tries for his partner, Smith. The last named showed that his tour in South Africa had taught him a lot for he ran with much more determination than formerly and in the first two matches actually scored eight times himself. Against neither Ireland nor England, however, did he rise to such heights. Of the four Aitken was the least conspicuous, but as partner to Wallace he proved invaluable, especially against Wales and Ireland.

Mention has been made of Waddell. Kept out of the first two games he came back with powers unimpaired and was the most dangerous stand-off half of the International season. Both at Dublin and Murrayfield he dropped goals to turn the matches for his side at critical times, but it was his strong individual play, whether in cutting through or in defence, that made him so pronounced a success. The loss of Bryce had seemed to be a great blow for

Scotland but in J. B. Nelson they discovered a scrum-half of equal skill. Nelson was the 'find' of the season and in not a single game did he play otherwise than brilliantly. Quick at the base of the scrum he got the ball out splendidly, while he was always dangerous near the line and possessed a hand-off nearly as effective as that of some of the giants of past days. For a comparatively little fellow his strength was remarkable. As substitute stand-off half Dykes played very well without attaining to great heights. He was unlucky. In ordinary circumstances he would have been Scotland's choice every time, but his best years have found him overshadowed by Waddell.

For their victories over Ireland and England, the Scotsmen probably owed most to the forwards. Certainly they did at Dublin where the Irish pack was outplayed just as the Irishmen themselves had had the best of the English forwards. Uniformly good was the work of D. J. MacMyn who, getting his cap at last, did a man's work in the scrummage and that of two in the loose. J. R. Paterson, of Birkenhead Park, was another great success, as were J. W. Scott and J. C. H. Ireland. Scott, a huge man, was consistency itself in every department of forward play, he and Gillies being very fine in the line-out and the loose. Bannerman as usual came through every match with flying colours, skill, allied to experience making him one of the outstanding forwards of the season, and Davies and Howie played very finely. Altogether Scotland in the end had a great side – well equipped at all points and real champions despite their close call against England.

REFLECTIONS

Norman Mair with Jimmy Ireland and Dan Drysdale

Jimmy Ireland, the Glasgow High School FP hooker, who was nine times on the winning side in gaining eleven caps for Scotland, recalls no talk of Triple Crown or Grand Slam in 1925: 'Herbert Waddell says that he can remember my remarking, after we had beaten Ireland, "Now for the Triple Crown", but I cannot claim to have any recollection of it whatsoever. The big thing in those days was to beat England and all the more so in 1925 in that England had won seven years in a row and nine out of the previous ten encounters.'

As a hooker, Ireland played in a transitional phase. Not only had 'First up, first down' passed into history but specialization had reached the point where the International Rugby Football Board's circular letter, which had been issued to players and referees in 1911 and revised in 1920 and 1925, actually contained a reference to the loose-head as such.

Scrum-halves, though, as Ireland reflects ruefully, did not always put the ball in on the loose-head, on occasion preferring to ensure that if the ball were won they would be moving on to the ball in the direction they would most likely want to pass.

'Another change in my time,' points out Ireland, a spry octogenarian by the year of Scotland's second Grand Slam, 'was that the wings took over the throwing-in at the line-out from the scrum-halves. Moreover, after Harry Stephenson scored a try for Ireland by a very quick and very short toss to himself, they brought in the five yards line. Previously, the throw did not have to travel five yards and the forwards could stand hard up against the touch-line.

'We did not block at the line-out in support of our main jumpers as they do today but there used to be one classic photograph in existence showing Scottish forwards in exemplary driving support of the jumper.'

'Feet, Scotland, feet!' was still a frequent battle-cry and the wheel much in evidence, both in attack and defence. In the former, the idea, of course, was to force an enemy back to go down on the ball and so give the Scottish backs a numerical advantage from the ensuing loose scrum.

'The all-important factor in the wheel,' notes Ireland, 'was to have a second row which was not only schooled and skilled in the tactic but very strong – and that, we had in John Bannerman and David MacMyn. Don't forget that, in defence, we always wheeled towards the touch-line and that, of course, often entailed wheeling against the loose-head.'

Dribbling was still an art. David MacMyn used to relate how he would practise for hours on end with his dog providing the most testing and frisky of opposition.

Ireland himself tells of how, for instance, much of the training at Old Anniesland, in those far-off days before flood-lights, consisted of games of soccer with a rugby ball in the enclosed space below the clubhouse. And of how one of the highlights of the year in Glasgow was the annual football match at Hampden between the Rugby Rovers and Queen's Park, then very much a power in the land.

Five of the pack could do the 100 yards in eleven seconds or better; namely, Ireland, Scott, MacMyn, Gillies and Paterson.

Interestingly, Ireland singles out Birkenhead Park's Scaley Paterson at wing forward as the outstanding player up front: small but ubiquitously mobile and a fine tackler. A key figure in a defence in which the tight forwards and the middle of the back row were expected to corner-flag indefatigably.

In his day, Ireland points out, Scotland teams would meet and travel on the Thursday for away matches but for home games assemble in Edinburgh only on the Saturday morning. Indeed, once, when he was employed by Singer in Glasgow, he asked if he could have the Saturday morning off because he would be playing for Scotland in Edinburgh in the after-noon. 'The whole morning?' responded his boss, doubtfully.

The contrast between that era and the intensity of approach in 1984 is captured exquisitely in Ireland's own and oft told tale of a journey through from Glasgow on the morning of an international. John Bannerman was holding forth on just what they would do to 'these bloody Irishmen'.

'But,' murmured Jimmy Ireland, 'it's Wales we are playing.'

'Well, bloody Welshmen then,' continued Bannerman.

Different days. Just how different can be judged from the fact that when Luddington of England opened the scoring in

1925 with a penalty goal – the first points ever notched at Murrayfield – it was the first penalty goal in the Calcutta Cup for thirty years.

A stand-off in his schooldays but switched to full-back by Heriot's FP, Dan Drysdale, who captained Scotland against Ireland in the 1925 Grand Slam, reckons that his first game for Scotland was only his seventh or eighth in the latter berth.

In all modesty, he thinks that he can fairly claim to have been ahead of his time in seeing the full-back as potentially the most dangerous of the outsides in attack in that he could choose his moment and place to come in, dictate many of his own attacking options and so often creep forward unobserved. Years later, the realm of Association Football similarly realized that an overlapping full-back would set the defence new problems regarding who was going to pick him up.

Drysdale, though, is quick to emphasize that, though he was always looking to come into the attack, he did not run the ball out of defence *à la* Andy Irvine simply because he had not been endowed with that kind of speed. Collectively, he still rates the Scotland backs of 1925 as the fastest back division he has ever seen; not necessarily in terms of track speed or even in a straight race from A to B in rugby boots but rather with regard to football speed, which is, as he says, compounded of many things and not least speed of thought, rugby nous and ball-sense. Drysdale insists that Ian Smith, who scored four tries in each of the first two internationals of 1925, and in six in succession, and who still holds the record for scoring the most tries in international rugby (with a haul of twenty-four), remains the fastest rugby player in this sense of football speed that he has known.

'Eric Liddell,' remembers Drysdale, 'looked tremendously fast even in rugby boots – and most certainly was – but I am convinced that Ian Smith, whose long, raking stride was deceptive if not entirely in the same way as Arthur Smith's more leisurely stride, was even swifter.

'Phil Macpherson was devastatingly quick and effective, able to go either way off either foot, a very great player. His fellow centre, the New Zealander, George Aitken, was considered by the rest of us in that side to be probably the best footballer of all, the John Dawes of his day, particularly in the sense that he tended to be under-estimated by many rugby folk.'

The other wing to Smith, Johnny Wallace – who shares the distinction with Catcheside of England and Esteve of France of having scored a try in each match of the International Championship in the one season – was, recalls Drysdale, 'Nowhere near as fast as Ian Smith but he had sturdy football sense and again a large ration of that priceless commodity of football speed.'

Drysdale, a devout believer in an established partnership at half-back – 'a feature common to virtually all great sides' – endorses the notion that the 1925 Grand Slam side owed a very great deal to the understanding at half-back of Jimmy Nelson, first with Jimmy Dykes and then, against Ireland and England, with Herbert Waddell, all three being Glasgow Academicals. 'Jimmy Nelson,' he ruminates, appreciatively, 'had a more than adequate service with a good length of pass and, besides suitable speed of foot, a punishing hand-off. He was very tough and, above all, had all the guts in the world.

'Herbert Waddell was something of a self-made player, though I say that more in admiration than in any derogatory sense. He wasn't naturally all that fast but he worked at it, training in spikes and so forth, and he made himself usefully quick over those vital first five or ten yards.

'I always thought his drop-kicking was better than his predominantly right-footed punting but his defence, like that of Nelson, was terrific. Any full-back would have had good cause to be grateful to both of them in that respect and another who could always be relied upon for tremendous tackling was Ian Smith. But then the defence of the backs generally was sound and the covering of the forwards good enough by the standards of what was expected of them in those days.'

As Drysdale readily confirmed, the Scottish backs of 1925 lay very much deeper than their counterparts in 1984 and they had lashings of confidence, one very good reason for which was the knowledge running through the whole back division that each knew how and when to pass. That ability, together with their footballing speed, had much to do with their being able to pierce or outflank even defences manning prepared positions at set scrums. It also helped provide the most extraordinary statistic of all to emanate from that historic season: that of the seventeen tries Scotland scored no fewer than fourteen were notched by the two wings.

In the opinion of most of the others in the 1925 side, Drysdale was, a little unexpectedly to my ears, the only authentically two-footed member of the team. In addition, he shared the goal-kicking with Sandy Gillies. Both, as was the fashion of the day, were toe-kickers.

Drysdale – who used to climb over the wall of the playing fields of what was then Merchiston Castle School to train with his sister, Anne, a hockey international in her own right – was the first in a line of eight international full-backs to come out of Goldenacre. That is a phenomenal achievement by one club and one which inspired what is still just about the best opening line in an after-dinner rugby speech I have yet encountered, that masterly orator, Arthur Stepney, declaring that he rose to speak, 'as one of that fast diminishing band of Herioters who have not yet played full-back for Scotland.'

12

The New Immortals

by Bill Lothian

PETER DODS
Full-back

FULL NAME Peter William Dods
BORN 6 January 1958 in Galashiels
CLUB Gala
OCCUPATION Joiner
HEIGHT 5 ft 8 in
WEIGHT 11 st 10 lb
EDUCATION Caddonfoot Primary School; Gala Academy
FIRST CAPPED v Ireland, 1983 at Murrayfield
MAJOR TOURS Scotland to France, 1980; Scotland to New
Zealand, 1981; Scotland to Australia, 1982; Scotland to
Rumania, 1984
STATUS Married, to Hazel with a daughter Lindsay
SCOTLAND RECORD won 5, drawn 1, lost 4. Points: 113, from
two tries, 27 penalties and 12 conversions

The rise and rise of Peter William Dods – the thirty-sixth Gala
player to be capped and the sixth from the Netherdale club to
play full-back for Scotland, following on from Borth Tod, Tom
Aitchison, George Burrell, Arthur Brown and Jock Turner – should
be an inspiration to all youngsters who struggle to make the grade
in their early rugby careers.

Dods failed to make a real impression in the Gala Academy sides
and it was with the semi-junior Gala Wanderers that he first started
to be noticed – as a winger. It was the non-appearance of a
colleague one day that meant a switch to full-back and led to South
semi-junior representative honours.

His first game for the Gala First XV, against Jedforest in 1975,
came at the age of seventeen and, although Dods wore the No. 15

A post-impact shot of the instep goal-kicking of Peter Dods as the Scotland full-back adds against England another penalty goal to his season's haul. *Bob Thomas*

shirt that day, he often alternated from game to game between wing and centre.

His preference, though, was always for full-back. When Arthur Brown obliged by moving to stand-off, the way became clear for Dods to establish himself, though it was in a game for the Gala Second XV that he excelled by slotting ten conversions out of ten from a variety of angles and distances.

Dods first wore the South jersey in 1978 against Cornwall (19–9) and Redruth and St Ives (24–6) during a two-match early season tour. By the beginning of the 1984–85 season, he had played 32 times for his district, including twice against New Zealand, and holds their points record with 303. His total in 169 games for Gala is 1,123.

Four B caps, a game against Holland for a Scottish Select and three overseas Scotland tours contributed to his apprenticeship before he won his first cap less than a fortnight after his twenty-fifth birthday.

On the Scotland tour of Australia Dods finished top scorer with 54 points from four games, adding to the 24 scored from four games in New Zealand the previous year.

Against Fiji in a non-cap encounter in September 1982, Dods claimed seventeen points from two tries, a penalty and three conversions, but it was not enough to give him the edge over Andy Irvine. However, Irvine went down injured again after the announcement of the team for the first championship fixture of 1983 and, although originally in by the back door, Dods has not been out since. His first international season yielded 33 points, not including five scored against the Barbarians, and Dods was soon chasing records.

Against the All Blacks in November 1983, he picked up fifteen points from the five penalties which kept pulling Scotland back from defeat. Dods went on to add seven points against Wales – kicking without a toe-cap in his right boot since it was separated early on from the sole – to help launch the Triple Crown bid, another ten against England and sixteen in Ireland. Those sixteen at Lansdowne Road equalled Andy Irvine's record individual haul for a Scot in a championship match.

Dods's first international try came versus Ireland and fittingly capped a famous win but he was to really surpass himself in the Grand Slam decider with France when his seventeen points, despite the handicap of a puffed right eye, enabled him to equal the best tally for a Scottish international, set by Andy Irvine against Australia at Murrayfield in 1982.

With his first kick of the match against France Dods passed Irvine's 1979–80 record of 35 points for Scotland in a championship series and he declared his innings temporarily closed at 50, having added another fifteen points in the 22–28 defeat in Rumania, including a memorable try to round off a truly brilliant handling move.

On the way to both his international touch-downs Dods revealed the type of pace which, in 1980, enabled him to collect a £300 prize and challenge cup for winning the coveted Jedforest sprint.

Dods's first kick in the Rumanian international enabled him to reach his century for Scotland and his admirable 113 points from ten appearances puts him second overall behind Irvine in the all-time list of Scottish points-scorers. He stands ahead of the like of I. S. Smith (72), K. J. F. Scotland (71), D. W. Morgan (71), S. Wilson (68), P. C. Brown (64), A. R. Smith (58), H. Waddell (45) and D. Drysdale (45), though it is worth noting that some of these totals would have been higher but for changes in the scoring values.

Reared in Clovenfords, where his father is a gamekeeper, Peter, the current Gala vice-captain, has a younger brother Michael, who represented Scotland at full-back in the first ever Under-15 international with Wales, at Meggetland in 1984. His wife, Hazel, is the daughter of Scotland cricket selector, Ian Crooks, and was a hockey player of district calibre with Gala Ladies until retiring to give birth to the couple's first child in September this year. Peter Dods's sporting pedigree also includes a grandfather who kept goal for the soccer side Gala Fairydean.

STEVE MUNRO
Right wing

FULL NAME Steven Munro
BORN 11 June 1958
CLUB Ayr
OCCUPATION Life Inspector
HEIGHT 5 ft 11 in
WEIGHT 13 st
EDUCATION Ayr Academy
FIRST CAPPED v Ireland, 1980 at Lansdowne Road
MAJOR TOURS Scotland to France, 1980; Scotland to New Zealand, 1981
STATUS Married, to Diane
SCOTLAND RECORD won 5, lost 5. Points: 8, from two tries

Steve Munro, the Ayr wing three-quarter, enjoys the rare distinction of having shared in Scottish victories in Wales at both school and senior level.

It was in 1976 that Munro, then a pupil at Ayr Academy, came off the replacements bench to help the Scottish Schools score a 9–7 victory over their Welsh counterparts at Llanelli. Though he could not officially be listed among the scorers, he was the player in possession when obstructed on the way to the line, a penalty try resulting.

The powerfully built Munro made his debut for the Ayr First XV against Perthshire in 1977 immediately after leaving school and represented Glasgow Under-23s before moving on to a full district berth in 1978 against North and Midlands. In 1979 Munro replaced the injured Matt Duncan for the B game with France at Millbrae, Ayr, which was never played on account of bad weather. Towards the end of that year, he was selected for Glasgow against the touring All Blacks and then for the Scotland B side which defeated their Irish counterparts 20–13 at Lansdowne Road.

After taking part in his first national trial in January 1980, Munro travelled to Aurillac to share in the 6–0 win of the Scotland B. A first cap was not long delayed, coming against Ireland in 1980 at Lansdowne Road when Scotland fell 15–22. He retained his place to share in the 22–14 triumph over France a fortnight later before temporarily dropping out of the limelight.

Munro came back to feature in all three matches in Scotland's 1980 short tour of France and went with Scotland to New Zealand, after a 1981 championship campaign distinguished by his two tries in the Calcutta Cup defeat at Twickenham. In New Zealand Munro played in six of the eight matches, including both Tests, and scored tries in the victories over Canterbury (23–12) and Mid Canterbury (23–12).

He lost his international place after the wet-weather win over Rumania in the autumn of 1981, by which time he had moved

Steve Munro. *Bob Thomas*

from Ayr, who had just been relegated to Division Three, to First Division West of Scotland. Ironically, it was not until returning to help Ayr in the first Division One stint that Munro made it back to the international scene. A useful display in the Whites' shock trial victory in January 1984 paved the way for a place in the side which visited Wales and won 15–9.

Though he was selected for the Calcutta Cup, an ankle injury cost him his Scotland berth and he was not selected for the Rumanian tour. Nevertheless the recall in Wales had enabled him to hoist his cap tally to ten.

Steve has three older brothers, none of whom play rugby. A keen squash player and twelve-handicap golfer, Munro switched jobs in 1984, moving from building society employment to become a life inspector with an insurance company.

In 1983 he toured the Carribean with the Saltires Select side.

JIM POLLOCK
Right wing

FULL NAME James Alan Pollock
BORN 16 November 1958
CLUB Gosforth
OCCUPATION Physical Education teacher
HEIGHT 5 ft 11 in
WEIGHT 12 st 5 lb
EDUCATION Linden Primary School; Foresthall; Newcastle Royal Grammar School
FIRST CAPPED v Wales, 1982 at Cardiff
MAJOR TOURS Scotland to Australia, 1982; Scotland to Rumania, 1984
STATUS Married, to Pamela
SCOTLAND RECORD won 5, drawn 1, lost 1. Points: 8 from two tries

A county schools representative in four sports while at Newcastle Royal Grammar School – rugby, cricket, water polo and athletics – Jim Pollock decided to concentrate on rugby, though the past summer has seen him performing in the Northumberland Lawn Tennis Championships and opening the bowling for Cramlington cricket club.

His captain at his feet, Jim Pollock changes direction as he backs up.
Dave Stranock

'Lucky Jim' is the nickname that has been hung on him – and little wonder remembering that it was not until his seventh Scotland appearance, against Rumania in Bucharest in May 1984, that he appeared in a losing Scotland team. Not only that but Pollock has the happy knack of scoring important tries, such as the late effort which enabled Scotland to achieve a 25–25 scoreline against New Zealand – the highest scoring draw in international history. It will be recalled, too, how he touched down on his debut – the 34–18 triumph over Wales – after he had been called into the team just the previous day when Keith Robertson was taken ill.

Scorer of the winning try when Northumberland celebrated their centenary season in 1981 by beating Gloucestershire in the English County Championship final at Twickenham (he was in the side beaten by Middlesex in 1979), Pollock marked his Scottish Inter-District Championship debut with two tries for the Anglos against the South at Roehampton in 1982. He played in ten successive Anglos matches until he missed the match against the South in 1983–84 through illness.

Coached at school by John Elders, the former England coach, Pollock joined the FP side, Old Novocastrians, for whom his older brother, Robert, still turns out at prop forward. He then moved on to Newcastle Northern, playing mainly at stand-off but, after it was suggested to him by the Northumberland coach, David Shaw, that his representative prospects would be improved playing on the wing, he moved along the road to Gosforth at the beginning of the 1981–82 season.

He is the son of Bill Pollock, a former Preston Lodge pupil and player. A couple of his international jerseys hang in his father's old club-house at Prestonpans. A graduate of Carnegie College, Leeds, Pollock presently teaches at Kenton Comprehensive School and it was from their playing fields that he was summoned to Cardiff for his Scotland debut.

That led to a tour of Australia, Pollock playing in five of the eight matches and scoring tries against New South Wales Country and Queensland Country. He played twice in Rumania.

Once a reserve for England Under-23s and selected for an England Student XV, he took nine wickets for 18 runs on one occasion in his schoolboy cricketing days. In athletics, he reached the final of the England Schools High Jump with a personal best of 5 feet 9 inches.

A Barbarian, he toured Canada with Northumberland in 1980.

ROGER BAIRD
Wing

FULL NAME Gavin Roger Todd Baird
BORN 12 April 1960 at Kelso
CLUB Kelso
OCCUPATION Grain Merchant
HEIGHT 5 ft 9 in
WEIGHT 12 st
EDUCATION St Mary's Preparatory School; Merchiston Castle
FIRST CAPPED v Australia, 1981 at Murrayfield
MAJOR TOURS Scotland to New Zealand, 1981; Scotland to Australia, 1982; British Lions to New Zealand, 1983
STATUS Single
SCOTLAND RECORD won 9, drawn 2, lost 5. Points: none

Roger Baird had the distinction of playing in three winning Scotland B teams, against Ireland (20–13) in 1979, France (6–0) in 1980 and France (18–4), again, in 1981.

Even more remarkable, by the time he had played twice for the South his First XV total appearances for his club, Kelso, numbered a mere one, against Glasgow Academicals. That was due to the fact that, in 1979, he had a late call to the Borderers party which toured Devon and Cornwall, his potential having been noted as a schoolboy in the Kelso seven. In fact, while at Merchiston, he collected a Melrose winners medal.

A measure of his progress can be gauged from the fact that by the start of the 1984–85 season, Baird had played 33 times for the South, scoring 22 tries, while he needed only Gala and Langholm winners medals to complete a Border sevens set.

Jean-Charles Orso smother tackled by an eager Roger Baird as Serge Blanco hovers expectantly. *Dave Stranock*

It was George Murray, the well known referee, who was the first to note Roger Baird's special talents at St Mary's, the preparatory school which has now produced 14 full internationals, including Willie Bryce, Tom and Arthur Dorward, Douglas Elliot, Tom Elliot, Gordon Waddell, Rodger Arneill, Ron Wilson, Alastair Biggar and Mike Biggar. At Merchiston, his rugby prowess was furthered by Peter Gait. In those days Baird was, of course, a scrum-half who represented the Scottish Schools twice.

Kelso put him on the wing in their crack seven and, with Bob Hogarth secure at scrum-half, it was virtually taken for granted that he would be converted to the role of wing three-quarter. Actually, much of last season was spent operating at centre for Kelso.

Sheer pace has always been one of his strongest attributes as he demonstrated by winning the Border 100, 200 and 400 metres titles on the same afternoon, although nowadays his main sporting pre-occupation, away from rugby, is golf. He has just been allocated his first national handicap, 21, at Luffness.

His father, Roger Baird senior, a Border vet, represented Watsonians, Kelso, Edinburgh and the South, besides getting within arms length of a cap. There are two other rugby-playing brothers in the family, Martin and Gareth, though neither has come near to reaching the levels of either Roger or their father. A Barbarian, who has also represented the Public School Wanderers and Co-optimists, the twenty-four-year-old Baird has taken part in the Hong Kong Bank/Cathay Pacific sevens on no fewer than four occasions.

Baird was close to a first cap on the 1981 Scottish tour of New Zealand when Steve Munro suffered a stomach virus during the build-up to the First Test. Munro recovered in time to play and during that trip Baird played just three games but scored two tries in the 38–9 rout of Marlborough at Blenheim between the two Tests.

By the time Scotland returned to the Southern Hemisphere in 1982, he was a full international and played in no fewer than six of the eight matches, scoring tries against New South Wales (31–7) and Capital Territories (22–4). In 1983 Baird toured New Zealand with the British Lions and the try he scored in the wet of Dunedin during the third of the four Tests remains his only international try to date. Playing in 11 of the 18 matches, including the four internationals, he proved he very definitely has an eye for the line by notching a total of six tries, making him joint second among try-scorers for the Lions on the tour.

KEITH ROBERTSON
Wing/Centre

FULL NAME Keith William Robertson
BORN 5 December 1954 at Hawick
CLUB Melrose
OCCUPATION Financial Consultant
HEIGHT 5 ft 11 in
WEIGHT 11 st
EDUCATION St Boswall's Primary School; Kelso High School
FIRST CAPPED v New Zealand, 1978 at Murrayfield
MAJOR TOURS Scotland to Far East, 1977; Scotland to France, 1980; Scotland to Australia, 1982; Scotland to Rumania, 1984
STATUS Married, to Alison with a daughter Nicola
SCOTLAND RECORD won 10, drawn 3, lost 14. Points: 26, from five tries and two drop goals

Keith Robertson has gained twenty of his caps as a wing and seven as a centre and is closing fast on Frank Laidlaw (32 caps) as the most capped Melrose player.

An established member of the Melrose side for the past ten years, he had a daunting debut in the centre, marking the international John Frame, of Gala, in 1974. Later that season Robertson, who has captained Melrose in three seasons, helped them win their own sevens trophy. The first representative honours for the Hawick-born Robertson, reared in Newton St Boswells, came with the South Under-21s against Cumberland at Carlisle as a centre. Robertson never really fulfilled his potential as a scrum-half at Kelso High School, growing too tall for the position.

In 1975 he was selected for a Scottish XV against Holland at Hilversum and later that year made his debut for the South against Australia at Netherdale. It was quite a year, in fact, for Robertson who also gained selection for a Scottish seven sent to a tournament in Ravehill, Belfast to mark the Irish Rugby Union centenary.

In 1976 he was picked for the 34–9 win over Japan at Murrayfield but he was not included in the Scotland XV which met the Japanese in Tokyo a year later, though he was on that tour of the Far East. One significant happening, so far as Robertson was concerned occurred, however, in 1978 when the South picked him on the wing against the Anglo-Scots. It was his first major outing

Keith Robertson. *George Herringshaw*

in that role and a month later he found himself lining up against New Zealand for his first cap and marking the legendary Bryan Williams.

The first of his five international tries came later that season against Ireland. In Rumania in 1984 he dropped his second goal to follow the one at Twickenham en route to the Calcutta Cup in 1983.

Unavailable to tour New Zealand in 1981 because his wife was expecting their first child, Robertson had a busy time of it on the 1982 tour of Australia, playing in the first five matches, including the two Tests, while it was his try in the 12–7 success at Brisbane which helped Scotland so much to their first Test win in the Southern Hemisphere.

Robertson underlined his unswerving loyalty to Melrose this year by flying from Rumania via London to Canada to link up for the final two matches of Melrose's first major overseas club tour.

The Scotland three-quarter has an older brother, John, who plays for Ruislip and, away from rugby, Keith's main interest is golf. In mid-1984, Robertson switched from the car sales business to become a financial consultant attached to a large insurance group.

DAVID JOHNSTON
Centre

FULL NAME David Ian Johnston
BORN 20 October 1958
CLUB Watsonians
OCCUPATION Solicitor
HEIGHT 5 ft 9 in
WEIGHT 10 st 7 lb
EDUCATION George Watson's College; Edinburgh University
FIRST CAPPED v New Zealand, 1979 at Murrayfield
MAJOR TOURS Scotland to France, 1980; Scotland to Australia, 1982; Scotland to Rumania, 1984
STATUS Married, to Michele
SCOTLAND RECORD won 10, drawn 2, lost 10. Points: 16, from four tries

David Johnston. *Bob Thomas*

Amazingly, David Johnston's first cap came after he had made only 29 appearances for Watsonians and played in just ten other senior games. When he entered the 1984–85 season with 22 caps to his credit, his total number of games for Watsonians numbered 98, with his try haul in club colours standing at 52. A remarkable ratio.

For a season on leaving school he had played soccer with Heart of Midlothian and may ultimately be remembered not least for using skills developed at Tynecastle to control an awkward bouncing ball and claim his fourth international try – the try which set Scotland on the way to 1984 Calcutta Cup glory against England.

Before signing with Hearts from Hutcheson Vale Boys Club, Johnston trained with Hibernian, Meadowbank Thistle and Glasgow Rangers but a foot injury and a certain degree of disillusionment with the Association code combined to point this former captain of both the Edinburgh and Scottish Schools sides back in the direction of the oval ball. Nevertheless, there can be few rugby caps who managed even one appearance in the Scottish League Division One – as Johnston did, against Dundee, in a 2–0 win. Willie Ormond was the Hearts manager in those days, arriving a few days after Johnston's signature had been procured by the coach, Bert Paton. His football career was only part-time, however, as Johnston continued his studies towards an honours degree in law.

Johnston gained a total of four Scottish Schools caps, leading the side against France in 1977. Once his rugby ambitions were reawakened, Johnston made his Watsonian debut against Tynedale and was quickly into the Edinburgh XV against New Zealand in 1979. His performance that day helped win him a place in the Scotland team which lost 6–20 against New Zealand a short time later. His championship debut in the 1980 match with Ireland at Lansdowne Road (15–22) was made all the more memorable by his two tries. Johnston played throughout that campaign and went on to the three-match tour of France, playing in every game.

Injury ruled him out of the 1981 championship and law examinations prevented him from touring New Zealand with Scotland. However, Johnston returned against Rumania in September 1981 and played throughout that season, scoring a classic try from an outside break in the 34–18 rout of Wales which preceded a Scottish tour of Australia in which he participated in both Tests. Immediately afterwards he visited South Africa with a World Invitation XV to celebrate the opening of the luxurious new Ellis Park in Johannesburg.

Dropped for a short span in 1983, Johnston gained his twenty-second cap in the 28–22 defeat by Rumania in Bucharest last May and also appeared in the opening 6–3 win over a Capital Select. At the start of the 1984–85 season, Johnston had made 25 appearances in the Edinburgh XV, including one on the wing against Kent, the position he occupied with distinction when playing for Scotland/Ireland against Wales/England at Cardiff in 1980.

The 1983–84 season saw Johnston's younger brother, Stuart, arrive on the district scene as a scrum-half and claim a place on the Scotland bench, filling the seat vacated by the injured Gordon Hunter. With Roy Laidlaw doubtful for the Rumanian tour up until the eleventh hour, it was touch and go whether the younger Johnston would join his brother on the plane.

David Johnston is grateful to Jimmy Cowan, a Watson's master, who converted him from wing to centre, and names Donald Scott, the former international on the staff of George Watson's College, as his other schoolboy rugby mentor.

He is the son of a former hockey player from Aberdeen, his mother hailing from south of the Border. Away from rugby his interests include skiing, golf and water-skiing.

EUAN KENNEDY
Centre

FULL NAME Alexander Euan Kennedy
BORN 30 July 1954 in Edinburgh
CLUB Watsonians
OCCUPATION Civil Engineer
HEIGHT 6 ft 5 in
WEIGHT 14 st
EDUCATION George Watson's College; Edinburgh University
FIRST CAPPED v New Zealand, 1983 at Murrayfield
MAJOR TOURS Scotland to Far East, 1977; Scotland to Rumania, 1984
STATUS Married, to Pamela with a son Scott
SCOTLAND RECORD won 2, drawn 1, lost 0. Points: 4, from one try

Euan Kennedy. *Bob Thomas*

The most striking feature about Alexander Euan Kennedy is un-doubtedly his height. At 6 ft 5 in, he stands taller than most of the Grand Slam forwards though he, of course, made his contribution at centre before being taken off with a damaged knee ligament early in the second half against England.

Immediately beforehand, Euan Kennedy, the fiftieth Watsonian First XV player to be capped, had crossed for his international try. With his fellow Myresider and co-centre, David Johnston, scoring earlier, the pair equalled the achievement of J. T. Simson and A. W. Angus, Watsonians who scored for Scotland in the same match back in 1911 against Ireland.

Kennedy, whose height goes with a solid frame, made his inter-national debut two matches before the England game when called upon to take over from the injured Keith Robertson. A shoulder injury had forced Robertson to pull out of the 25–25 draw with New Zealand early in the week. Kennedy then retained his place for the visit to Wales at the start of the championship.

Though centre was his position during a schoolboy career which was not distinguished by representative honours, he was forced to switch to full-back on joining the Watsonian club, the Scottish international David Bell and the accomplished Douglas Neave barring the way in his preferred role.

He took the move in his stride and progressed to a Scottish Under-21 cap in 1974 while in 1975 he travelled to Hilversum with the Young Scotland XV which met Holland. Scotland won 29–3 and Kennedy contributed eleven points from a try, two conversions and a penalty.

A few months later, Kennedy made his district debut against Nice under the Meadowbank floodlights. Although he scored ten points in a 30–7 win, it was to prove his only game at full-back for an Edinburgh side he has captained on nine of his 26 appearances, going into the 1984–85 season. His total points in Edinburgh colours is just three short of the half-century.

In 1976 Kennedy, with his two district rivals, Bruce Hay and Andy Irvine, both ineligible, earned his first B cap against France at Rheims and, before switching back to centre in 1978–79, he went with Scotland to the Far East, kicking 23 points in an 82–3 win over Thailand.

Though captain of the Scotland B against France at Ayr in 1981, Kennedy was left out of the full squad's tour party for New Zealand later that same year and likewise the trip to Australia in 1982. But around that period he must have been extremely close to a first cap, for he was selected to represent the Blues in a final Scotland trial. At half-time, though, he was required to switch over to the Whites XV.

Aided by an individual haul of 30 points against Hillhead – also a club record for one match – Kennedy, by the start of the 1984–85 season, had scored 827 points from 203 games in Watsonian First XV colours, considerably more than the previous record of 667 achieved by A. W. Angus between 1906 and 1921.

Son of Dr Gilbert Kennedy, a former Scotland trialist, Euan Kennedy had the honour of leading Watsonians at the same time as his father was serving as president. His brothers, Billy, now with London Scottish, and Gordon, are both useful forwards who have worn the maroon and white of Watsonians on many occasions and, coincidentally, Billy also made an Edinburgh debut against Nice, in France.

Euan is employed as a civil engineer with Lothian Regional Council.

JOHN RUTHERFORD
Stand-off

FULL NAME John Young Rutherford
BORN 4 October 1955 in Selkirk
CLUB Selkirk
OCCUPATION Building Society Representative
HEIGHT 6 ft 1 in
WEIGHT 12 st
EDUCATION Philiphaugh Primary School; Selkirk High School;
Jordanhill College of Physical Education
FIRST CAPPED v Wales, 1979 at Murrayfield
MAJOR TOURS Scotland to Far East, 1977; Scotland to France,
1980; Scotland to New Zealand, 1981; Scotland to Australia,
1982; British Lions to New Zealand, 1983; Scotland to
Rumania, 1984
STATUS Married, to Alison
SCOTLAND RECORD won 12, drawn 4, lost 12. Points: 45, from
six tries and seven drop goals

John Rutherford is Scotland's most capped stand-off, his 28 caps
up to the 1984–85 season being well in excess of the eighteen won
by Gordon Waddell between 1957 and 1962. Never dropped by
Scotland since making his debut against Wales at Murrayfield in
1979, he could not, however, be considered because of injuries for
the matches against Wales in 1980 and 1983; Rumania in 1981;
and both Ireland and France in 1983.

A former Physical Education master at George Watson's College,
but now an executive with the Bristol and West Building Society,
Rutherford scored for Scotland in each of his five appearances in
the 1981–82 season and has touched down on all of the grounds
used for Five Nations Championship matches except Cardiff. His
international points tally at the beginning of the 1984–85 season
was 45, comprising six tries and seven drop goals. The only other
player to have dropped seven goals for Scotland is Ian McGeechan.

His international partnership with Roy Laidlaw is so well established that in Rumania in May 1984 they equalled the world record
of Gareth Edwards and Barry John for a half-back combination
of 23 appearances together.

In 1983 John Rutherford toured New Zealand with the British
Lions and was introduced as a centre in the Third Test. Rutherford
scored a try in that match but a groin injury ruled him out of the

John Rutherford. *Bob Thomas*

Fourth Test and he was limited, overall, to ten games out of a possible eighteen.

A spell on the injured list upon his return was particularly galling because Rutherford had been compelled to undergo surgery less than a year earlier. A steel pin had been inserted in his shoulder after he had stayed on the field in Selkirk's national league fixture with Gordonians, even though muscle had become detached from the bone. Selkirk's sixth international, following on from Willie Bryce, Jack Watters, Basher Inglis, Jock King and Ronnie Cowan, is, not unnaturally, among the staunchest of advocates that replacements should be permitted for an injured player in Scottish club rugby.

His first appearance in a Selkirk jersey came in 1973 when, still a schoolboy, he scored three tries against Glasgow Academicals in the first round of a Gala sevens tournament which had been held back to May, because of the SRU's Centenary Sevens at Murrayfield in early April. A schoolboy international, he made his First XV debut for Selkirk in 1973 against Langholm, after graduating through the prolific Selkirk Youth Club ranks.

By the end of the 1983–84 season, John Rutherford had played 30 times for the South, captaining them on ten occasions, including the match against Fiji in 1982. His district career began against Australia at Netherdale in December 1975.

In addition to playing against all the leading rugby countries, except South Africa, Rutherford has twice played for Scottish Selects against Holland – at Hughenden in 1974 and at Hilversum in 1975 when he scored a try playing at centre. He was a B international against Ireland in 1977 and France in 1978, his first trial appearance being immediately prior to his debut cap in 1979. During his international career he has been partnered by just three scrum-halves, Roy Laidlaw, Alan Lawson and his Selkirk colleague Gordon Hunter, who came on as a replacement in Dublin in 1984.

Voted Scotland's top performer in 1980 by readers of *Rugby World* magazine, John has a younger brother, Billy, who was in the Selkirk team which won their own sevens tournament in 1982, and an older brother James, who does not play. Billy is currently vice-captain of Peebles RFC.

Keenly interested in soccer and a former captain of his school cricket XI, John Rutherford is a member of Merchant's Golf Club in Edinburgh. John's wife, Alison, is a former Scotland Under-23 and B hockey cap. The couple actually met on the terracing of the National Stadium, Wales, during an international rugby match in 1976. This year both realized a long-standing ambition by visiting the Olympic Games, in Los Angeles.

Despite settling in Edinburgh, Rutherford has captained Selkirk four times and also served them as coach. Just prior to his first cap, Rutherford cited Jock King, the Selkirk cap, as the 'biggest influence' on his career. Others who have helped in his development include John Torrie, who coached primary schoolboys in the town, Harry Russell and Bill Dickinson.

ROY LAIDLAW
Scrum-half

FULL NAME Roy James Laidlaw
BORN 5 October 1953 in Jedburgh
CLUB Jedforest
OCCUPATION Electrician
HEIGHT 5 ft 7 in
WEIGHT 11 st 7 lb
EDUCATION Parkside Primary; Jedburgh Grammar Schools

FIRST CAPPED v Ireland, 1980 at Lansdowne Road
MAJOR TOURS Scotland to Far East, 1977; Scotland to France,
1980; Scotland to New Zealand, 1981; Scotland to Australia,
1982; British Lions to New Zealand, 1983; Scotland to
Rumania, 1984
STATUS Married, to Joy with sons Scott and Clark
SCOTLAND RECORD won 13, drawn 2, lost 13. Points: 16, from
four tries

Captain of Jedforest for a fifth time in their 1984–85 centenary
season, Roy Laidlaw, appropriately enough, became the Riverside
Park club's only British Lion when he toured New Zealand in
1983, playing a full part in the last three Test matches after
replacing the injured Terry Holmes 29 minutes into the opening
international.

On that Lions tour, Laidlaw shared with the Welsh prop, Staff
Jones, the record number of appearances, thirteen out of a possible
eighteen, and had the pleasure of leading the side to their two

Roy Laidlaw dive-passing as the Welsh captain, Eddie Butler, takes aim on
the Scottish mid-field. *Bob Thomas*

biggest victories, Wairarapa Bush (57–10) and West Coast (52–16).

Although captain of a 'Lion-less' Scotland on their 1980 short tour of France and at the helm when they beat Fiji by 32–12 at Murrayfield in September 1982, Laidlaw was unable to inspire the side to victory when he was invested with the captaincy for the opening three championship fixtures of 1983, at home to Ireland (13–15) and Wales (15–19) and away to France (15–19).

That particular Irish match, the first full international to be played in front of the new £3 million Murrayfield East stand, saw Laidlaw notch the first of his international tries. Once released from the pressures of the captaincy he responded with the opening try when Scotland rounded off their 1983 championship campaign by winning the Calcutta Cup at Twickenham for only the second time since the war.

Matches against Ireland must have a special place in Laidlaw's heart. He was awarded his first cap against them in 1980 and it was a two-try display in a B team victory on the same Lansdowne Road pitch a few weeks previously which had clinched his promotion after he had been thirteen times a replacement and seven times a member of Scotland B.

Laidlaw's proudest moment came on 3 March 1984 when, on that lush Dublin sward, he overtook the 25-times capped Glasgow Academical, Jimmy Nelson, as Scotland's record holder at scrum-half. What is more, he celebrated in style with a brace of early tries from set-pieces which doubled his international tally and set Scotland up for the Triple Crown. Laidlaw failed to finish the match, for a second time in Scotland colours, because of a head knock (he was withdrawn at Cardiff in 1980). He recovered to hoist his cap tally by the end of the 1983–84 season to 28.

Coincidentally, like Jimmy Nelson, his caps have been gained consecutively. A further twist is that Nelson made his debut in 1925 – Scotland's last Grand Slam year!

In Rumania in May 1984, Laidlaw equalled a world record of 23 appearances in the company of the same stand-off – John Rutherford. The record previously stood solely in the name of the Welsh pair, Gareth Edwards and Barry John.

Introduced to rugby at Jedburgh Grammar School, though not to representative level, Laidlaw played until 1970 with the semi-junior Jed Thistle. He then graduated to the senior team where he was frequently utilized as a stand-off while his debut, against Edinburgh University, was one of only two games played as a centre.

A member of the South semi-juniors XV, he earned district spurs on 10 October 1973 when Durham County were defeated 18–9 at Blaydon. By the end of the 1983–84 season, Laidlaw had represented his district 52 times, having completed his half-century against North Midlands under the Kelso floodlights on a bitterly cold December evening, once again revealing a penchant for celebrating momentous occasions with a try.

Laidlaw's South career includes matches against Argentina (1973), Australia (1975), New Zealand (1979 and 1983), Fiji (1982) and the South African Barbarians. He led the South to an inter-district clean sweep in 1982–83. In addition to visiting New Zealand twice, Laidlaw has toured Australia, France and the Far East with Scotland squads, scoring two tries in the 74–9 rout of Japan in Tokyo in September 1977.

In all, he has faced the All Blacks nine times, having played in both Tests on Scotland's 1981 tour and the home engagement at Murrayfield earlier in the Grand Slam season. He has, he notes ruefully, yet to enjoy a win!

The eighth Jedforest player to be capped, he follows on from J. T. Mabon, Dr J. L. Huggan, George Douglas, Bill Purdie, Charlie McDonald, David Rose and Hugh Duffy. It is a measure of his affection for the town which has honoured him as their Sportsman of the Year on several occasions that he counts among his prize possessions a Melrose seven-a-side medal won with his club in 1974, a year before they triumphed in their own 'Sports'. He was also, incidentally, captain of the Jedforest team which gained promotion to Division One for the first time, in 1980–81.

While at Jedburgh Grammar, Laidlaw came under the rugby influence of Bill Johnston but he reckons his first actual coach was Rod Sharp, who would devote hours to providing primary school children with basic rugby skills. George 'Papa' Forbes (Jed Thistle), Charlie Murdoch, Jim Thomson, Jim McDonnell and Alan Goodfellow are other coaches singled out by Laidlaw, the middle of three rugby-playing brothers. David is a utility back, also with Jedforest, while John is a wing with Corstorphine.

Away from rugby, Laidlaw has a keen interest in pigeon racing and, having won a junior trophy earlier in life, hopes to return to that sport once his playing days are over.

His rugby pedigree comes mainly from his paternal grandfather, who played on the wing for both Langholm and Jedforest.

GORDON HUNTER
Scrum-half

FULL NAME Iain Gordon Hunter
BORN 7 August 1958
CLUB Selkirk
OCCUPATION Chartered Surveyor
HEIGHT 5 ft 10 in
WEIGHT 12 st 4 lb
EDUCATION James Gillespie's Primary School; Royal High School; Heriot Watt University
FIRST CAPPED v Ireland, 1984 at Lansdowne Road
MAJOR TOURS Scotland to New Zealand, 1981; Scotland to Australia, 1982; Scotland to Rumania, 1984
STATUS Married, to Nancy
SCOTLAND RECORD won 1, drawn 0, lost 0. Points: none

Although educated at Edinburgh's illustrious Royal High School rugby nursery, where he came under the influence of Douglas Mitchell and played for the Scottish Schools in the 50–7 defeat by France in 1976, Gordon Hunter was actually born in Hawick and lived in Selkirk until aged five. Hawick have yet to have a capped scrum-half though had Gordon Hunter's father Ronald, a former Hawick YM wing, stayed put then he would have been the first.

Hunter sat fifteen matches on the Scotland bench, always understudying Roy Laidlaw, and played in four B internationals, captaining the B side against France at Dundee in 1983, before his great chance came with Scotland leading 22–0 in the Triple Crown match with Ireland. Laidlaw retired at half-time and Gordon came on to deputize. His ecstacy at full-time was quickly muted, though, when he collided with a spectator while running off the field and suffered a depressed cheekbone fracture similar to the one he sustained against Wellington which put him out of Scotland's New Zealand tour in 1981.

As Bill Dickinson, the former Scotland 'adviser to the captain', and Hunter's mentor at Selkirk in recent years, remarked later, 'Gordon's luck must be changing. I'd have expected him to have collided with the spectator *before* he got on for his cap.'

In 1982 Hunter went with Scotland to Australia and, as in New Zealand a year earlier, scored a try in the opening match, going on to play four games altogether.

Gordon Hunter dive-passing versus Ireland. *All Sport*

He made his Selkirk debut in 1976 against Allan Glen's FP and appeared for the first time in South colours against Connaught on the Irish tour of 1980. The 1983–84 inter-district championship saw him displace his old rival, Roy Laidlaw, for a spell and he was included in the Blues team for the national trial.

Spring training under the celebrated athletics coach Wilson Young has helped his progress and there have been times, too, when his wife, Nancy, has been detailed to line-up at stand-off as Gordon sought to lengthen his passing.

Gordon, who has an older brother, James, who plays rugby in the Army, worked until mid-1984 with a large insurance company in Edinburgh, travelling every day from the house which he built in Ashkirk, near Selkirk. Then he moved to a post in Galashiels alongside the former Gala president Frank Entwhistle. Horse-riding and golf are among Hunter's interests away from rugby.

JIM AITKEN
Loose-head prop

FULL NAME James Aitken
BORN 22 November 1947 in Penicuik
CLUB Gala
OCCUPATION Managing Director of a grain company
HEIGHT 5 ft 11 in
WEIGHT 15 st 9 lb
EDUCATION Cuiken Primary School; Penicuik High School;
Edinburgh College of Commerce
FIRST CAPPED v England, 1977 at Twickenham
MAJOR TOURS Scotland to New Zealand, 1981; Scotland to
Australia, 1982; Scotland to Rumania, 1984
STATUS Married, to Ruth with sons Neil and Russell
SCOTLAND RECORD won 13, drawn 2, lost 11. Points: 4, from
one try

Only once on a losing team at Murrayfield – against Wales in 1983
– in a 26-cap international career, Jim Aitken was a wing forward
with Penicuik when, in 1971, he sought out a higher level of rugby
with Gala. He had been pointed in the direction of Netherdale,
once his mind was made up, by Billy Easson, a former Gala centre
who served on the Penicuik committee.

After one game at No. 8 for the Gala Second XV, Aitken found
himself at loose-head for them against Jedforest the next week.
Seven days later, it was loose-head against West Hartlepool for the
First XV and from there he has scarcely looked back.

Since that debut, in fact, Aitken had played 297 games for
Gala up to the start of the 1984–85 season, scoring 12 tries and
captaining them to two of their three Scottish Championships and
four times in all.

In only his second season at Netherdale, Aitken merited a Scottish trial and made his South debut against the North and Midlands,
taking advantage of the retirement of the Hawick cap, Norman
Suddon. By the end of the Grand Slam campaign, Aitken had
played 53 more games for the South, though influenza caused him
to miss last October's clash with Stu Wilson's touring All Blacks.
Aitken captained the South on eight occasions including their
1983–84 inter-district Grand Slam.

He was first honoured with the Scotland captaincy against

Canterbury (23–12) on the 1981 tour of New Zealand. A year later, in Australia, he captained the side against New South Wales Country (44–3) and Capital Territory (22–4). In between those two matches came the First Test, for which Aitken was dropped in favour of West's Gerry McGuinness, Aitken having gained twelve caps consecutively since the 1981 French encounter. It was the second time Aitken had been discarded by his country.

Following B caps in 1975 (when a certain Jean-Pierre Rives was in the French ranks) and 1976, Aitken made his debut in a record 26–6 Calcutta Cup defeat at Twickenham in 1977, the fourth Gala prop to be capped post-war, following Bob Wilson, John Fox and Tom Elliot. Bob Cunningham joined that list a little later.

His club's thirty-first international, Aitken played against Ireland and France, also in 1977, before giving way to the man he had deposed, Ian McLauchlan. He remained in the international wilderness until recalled for the 1981 championship and, after being dropped for McGuinness in Australia a year later, 'Big Daddy' proved he was made of durable material by shrugging aside thoughts of retirement to soldier on.

Your captain calling . . . *George Herringshaw*

A place on the bench against Fiji was an inauspicious start to the season that was to end with his name on the Calcutta Cup as the winning captain. It was only the 15–13 defeat by Ireland at the start of the championship which persuaded the selectors to put their trust in him again.

After Twickenham and Scotland's second post-war Calcutta Cup win at RFU headquarters, Aitken went so far as to indicate his retirement, though staying in training on stand-by as a reserve for the Lions in New Zealand. On reflection, he decided it would be a shame to waste his summer fitness and his captaincy encouraged Scotland to come back from a seven-points deficit three times before snatching a 25–25 draw with the All Blacks at Murrayfield in November 1983.

The national trial in which the Whites beat the Blues, or senior side, 21–3 helped to clear up certain problem areas with regard to the Scottish team for the opening match in Wales, where Aitken's first international try provided the springboard to Triple Crown and Grand Slam glory.

In the wake of the Triple Crown, Aitken expressed a desire to try to become the first Scottish captain to lead his side to victory on all five championship grounds – a win in Paris in 1985 being required for the set. He saw his unbeaten record as Scotland captain go in Bucharest in May when, in a temperature of 91 degrees, the side lost 22–28 to Rumania. It was Aitken's 24th cap, his seventh as international captain.

A Managing Director of a grain firm whose turnover has risen from £3¾ million to £9 million during his five years, Jim Aitken is the son of a former Army hockey player and his younger brother, David, is currently captain of Penicuik, the club Jim helps to coach.

COLIN DEANS
Hooker

FULL NAME Colin Thomas Deans
BORN 3 May 1955 at Hawick
CLUB Hawick
OCCUPATION Tyre company manager
HEIGHT 5 ft 10 in
WEIGHT 13st 4 lb
EDUCATION Trinity Primary School; Hawick High School

FIRST CAPPED v France, 1978 at Murrayfield
MAJOR TOURS Scotland to Far East, 1977; Scotland to France,
1980; Scotland to New Zealand, 1981; Scotland to Australia,
1982; British Lions to New Zealand, 1983
STATUS Married, to Valerie with sons Rodney and Ross
SCOTLAND RECORD won 13, drawn 4, lost 17. Points: 4, from
one try

Colin Thomas Deans, whose father, Peter, hooked for Hawick
before him and also captained the club, probably savoured Scotland's Grand Slam more than most.

After four B caps, starting against France in 1976 at Rheims, he
came into the international arena as a 22-year-old and then had
to wait just over two years and ten further matches before enjoying
a win.

In fact, that elusive victory did not occur until France's next visit
to Edinburgh and even then Deans took only a limited part in the
fray, retiring because of rib cartilage damage after just 20 minutes

Dubbed the best torpedo throw outside the domain of American football, the
spiralling line-out toss of Colin Deans. *Bob Thomas*

and long before Andy Irvine galvanized the Scots into a never-to-be-forgotten fightback which saw a 4–14 deficit transformed into a late 22–14 triumph.

On the sidelines for the two remaining matches that season, Deans took until the Triple Crown joust with Ireland to pass another Borderer, Frank Laidlaw (32 caps), as Scotland's most capped hooker. Unavailable to tour Rumania due to family commitments, he finished the 1984 season on the 34-cap mark.

Colin Deans, no relation to Derek Deans, is now in his second term as club captain and led Scotland against a French Select at Brive during the short 1980 tour. He also toured the Far East in 1977, playing in the 74–9 win over Japan as well as against New Zealand in 1981 and Australia a year later.

In 1983 he became Hawick's tenth British Lion, returning to New Zealand, but he was forced to understudy the captain, Ciaran Fitzgerald, in all four Tests. Deans figured in a total of seven provincial games, including the one against Canterbury, and scored tries versus Hawkes Bay (25–19) and Waikato (40–13).

He began the 1984–85 season just one match short of a fiftieth appearance in South district colours and with eleven tries at that level to his credit since making his debut in 1974. His only international try so far was scored in the 11–4 defeat by New Zealand in the First Test of the 1981 tour.

Fast enough around the field to have been encouraged in his formative years to consider playing centre, Deans owes much of his pace to summer training with professional sprinters; among them his elder brother, Stuart, a winger with Hawick YM, and his brother-in-law, Colin Turnbull.

At Hawick High School, Deans struggled to command a regular place and his semi-junior rugby was played with Hawick Wanderers – whom his father has served as president – and he was once selected for representative duty at that level as a No. 8.

By the time he joined Hawick Trades, he was firmly committed to playing hooker, his first game for Hawick coming shortly afterwards against Ballymena in September 1973. An Under-21 cap followed and two years later he was picked for a Scottish Select which visited Holland.

Colin Deans has two sons, Rodney and Ross, the latter born while the Lions were in New Zealand. Deans occasionally plays golf but gives his main alternative recreation as gardening.

In a coaching sense, Deans is indebted to Derrick Grant and Jim Telfer, and acknowledges that Johnny Gray of Gala, in his capacity as South coach, has also been of great assistance.

IAIN MILNE
Tight-head prop

FULL NAME Iain Gordon Milne
BORN 17 June 1958 in Edinburgh
CLUB Heriot's FP and Harlequins
OCCUPATION Assitant Manager of printing works
HEIGHT 6 ft
WEIGHT 16 st 5 lb
EDUCATION Blackhall Primary School; George Heriot's; Heriot Watt University
FIRST CAPPED v Ireland, 1979 at Murrayfield
MAJOR TOURS Scotland to New Zealand, 1981; Scotland to Australia, 1982; British Lions to New Zealand, 1983
STATUS Single
SCOTLAND RECORD won 11, drawn 3, lost 10. Points: none

The Bear on the run. Iain Milne prepares to meet the challenge of Mark Douglas. *Bob Thomas*

A popular recent quiz question concerns which front-rank rugby club is able to field three brothers in their front row?

The answer is to be found at Goldenacre where Heriot's FP sent Iain, Kenneth and David Milne out on to the field virtually every Saturday of 1984, except when injury struck or representative duties beckoned.

By far the most experienced of the three brothers is Iain, the first Heriot's prop to be capped and their sixth British Lion, following on from Dan Drysdale, Kelly Hendrie, Roy Kinnear, Ken Scotland and Andy Irvine. Unavailable to tour Rumania with Scotland last May, Milne entered the 1984–85 season with 24 caps to his credit, his potential first being rewarded by the Edinburgh Schools selectors in 1973.

In his first year out of school, Milne made his senior debut in a national league game and remembers that it was against Dunfermline, mainly because that happened to be the Fifers' only victory in the First Division that season.

When Iain, son of Dr Kenneth Milne, a former hockey player, emerged to challenge for a Heriot's First XV spot, Jim Burnett moved over from tight-head to loose-head. It was a profitable transfer for, three matches after Milne's cap debut, Burnett was included in the Scottish team for four matches in 1980. Not bad for someone who once lay in a hospital bed suffering the trauma of a broken neck.

While Burnett's caps came late in his career, Milne was only twenty-one when he first appeared in a Scottish jersey, without having played for the B Fifteen. Milne's debut cap was in an 11–11 draw with Ireland and he has been a regular member of the side save when injury forced him to miss the 1981 championship. He was, though, unable to go on Scotland's 1980 tour of France.

Particularly proud of having been a member of the Heriot's side which won their first official Scottish championship in 1979 and also in the side which won the now moribund Bass Charrington Trophy at Wembley, Iain Milne captained Heriot's from 1981 to 1983. Milne's district career with Edinburgh now extends to 38 matches, having begun against North and Midlands in 1975.

Nicknamed the 'Bear' on account of his bulk and propping technique, Iain played in five games on Scotland's 1981 tour of New Zealand and an identical number in Australia a year later where he notched his only try to date for Scotland – against New South Wales (31–7). In New Zealand with the Lions, he played in eight provincial matches and scored a try against Waikato.

A former captain of Edinburgh Under-23s, he lists the Heriot's

PE master, Stuart Barnes, as a notable influence on his career after he had switched from hooker to prop in his second year. He says that later on John Stent, Iain Lawrie and Peter Hill gave him considerable aid.

Away from rugby, Milne enjoys fishing and occasional golf, though he does not possess a national handicap.

BILL CUTHBERTSON
Lock

FULL NAME William Cuthbertson
BORN 6 December 1949 at Kilwinning
CLUB Harlequins
OCCUPATION Company Representative
HEIGHT 6 ft 3 in
WEIGHT 15 st 7 lb
EDUCATION Troon Primary School; Marr College
FIRST CAPPED v Ireland, 1980 at Lansdowne Road
MAJOR TOURS Scotland to New Zealand, 1981; Scotland to Australia, 1982
STATUS Married, to Alana with a daughter Lyn and a son Gregor
SCOTLAND RECORD won 8, drawn 2, lost 8. Points: none

Bill Cuthbertson, an Ayrshireman who now lives in Camberley, came on to the international scene comparatively late. He was 31 when he earned his debut cap against Ireland in 1980 at a time when a regular Scotland lock, Alan Tomes, was under suspension following an ordering off. Tomes returned for the subsequent match but Cuthbertson was not to be lastingly discarded, embarking on a run of 16 successive caps from the Welsh visit to Murrayfield in 1981 to March 1983 when he was omitted from the team which won the Calcutta Cup at Twickenham.

Cuthbertson, or 'Gulliver' to his friends on ironic account of an intense dislike of travelling, refused to be written off then and contributed to the historic 1983–84 season by playing against New Zealand and Wales before being injured during the win over England and replaced at half-time by John Beattie.

A former centre-half with Ardeer Recreation FC, Cuthbertson was duly selected for the Triple Crown game in Ireland but his

Chair-lift. Bill Cuthbertson wins a line-out deflection against Wales under the approving gaze of his captain, Jim Aitken. *George Herringshaw*

groin injury failed to respond to treatment in time and, to his great disappointment, he was left out of the squad which went to Rumania in May. Cuthbertson, who enjoys being regarded as team 'choir-master' while on tour, had the satisfaction of visiting New Zealand and Australia with Scotland, playing in all the internationals. He has also been to Canada with Middlesex.

It was while in New Zealand that the story emerged of how the hosts, through the medium of an eavesdropper bringing out the oranges, were carrying out a survey on what was said at half-time talks. The upshot was that Cuthbertson came to be regarded as the Scot with the most analytical mind.

In addition to leading Scotland against Victoria (38–3) at Olympic Park, Melbourne on the Australian tour, Cuthbertson has captained the Barbarians against Cardiff during an Easter tour. He has also captained the Anglos on five occasions and the Glasgow team for whom he made his debut as recently as 1977, against the South at Hughenden, at the age of 28. He has also been captain of Kilmarnock.

He recalls being a regular Glasgow reserve for several years while playing with Marr College FP but, in his first season after moving on to Kilmarnock, the selectors finally decided to give him his chance.

Winning a national league game at Gala in Kilmarnock colours represents another career highlight for a man who once held a golf handicap of four at Old Troon but who finds he now has only limited opportunities to play golf, living as he does in the London area.

During his early days with Glasgow, Cuthbertson reckoned both Ian McLauchlan and Ritchie Dixon helped him enormously, and, further back, he is indebted to Keir Hardie, Arthur Dunsmuir and Tony McGuffie for their coaching at Marr. Twice a B international, Cuthbertson first saw representative action as an Ayrshire Schools No. 8 and also played for the Glasgow Juniors XV before making his Marr debut against Old Spierans.

He is a fitter by trade but his move south in 1982 took him into selling. In July 1984 he took up new employment with a roofing company.

ALAN TOMES
Lock

FULL NAME Alan James Tomes
BORN 6 November 1951 at Hawick
CLUB Hawick
OCCUPATION Gas Board Executive
HEIGHT 6 ft 5 in
WEIGHT 17 st
EDUCATION Hawick High School Primary; Heathfield Grammar School, Gateshead
FIRST CAPPED v England, 1976 at Murrayfield
MAJOR TOURS Scotland to New Zealand, 1975; Scotland to Far East, 1977; British Lions to South Africa, 1980; Scotland to New Zealand, 1981; Scotland to Australia, 1982; Scotland to Rumania, 1984
STATUS Married, to Sheena with a daughter Sally and son Sean
SCOTLAND RECORD won 14, drawn 3, lost 21. Points: 12, from three tries

Alan Tomes, or 'Toomba' to his rugby friends, worked hard to revive his international career in the Grand Slam season. He was on the side-lines when the All Blacks visited Murrayfield and left with a 25–25 draw, but he got the vote over his great rival, Tom Smith, for the hazardous journey to Wales.

Tomes played his part that day and swam with the tide thereafter, earning his thirty-eighth cap in Rumania in May 1984, to stand just four behind the record for a Scottish lock of 42 held by Alastair McHarg. McHarg did, however, make another two international appearances as a No. 8.

Tomes also finished the Grand Slam season chasing the international try record for a Scottish forward which is four. His mobility, unexpected in such a big fellow, brought him tries against Wales in 1978 and 1981 and against England in 1980.

Alan Tomes. *Bob Thomas*

It will be remembered, too, that he was up in support to mark his international debut, against England in 1976, with a scoring pass to Alan Lawson in a marvellous break-out score – an achievement he repeated when Jim Calder crossed for the opening try in the 34–18 rout of Wales in 1982. It was Tomes who put him in possession a few yards out after Roger Baird had instigated the attack and Iain Paxton had continued it.

Tomes is used to 'trekking' in another sense. In 1959, along with his mother and father, Charlie, a former Hawick Harlequins player and official, he went to live on Tyneside and he is still there. His early senior rugby was played with Gateshead Fell but Alan, although he has a county cap in Durham, never forgot his Hawick background, making his debut for them against Northumberland in September 1973.

He made his South debut against Durham in 1974 and was taken, uncapped, by the Scotland party to New Zealand in 1975, playing in three matches. The following year he went with the Barbarians to Canada and the USA, by which time he was a fully fledged international.

Though being sent off in a district game between the South and Edinburgh at Goldenacre in December 1979 cost him a cap against Ireland in early 1980, Tomes played in the remainder of that year's championship to merit inclusion in the British Lions team which toured South Africa: one of five Scots originally chosen. He made seven provincial appearances on that tour.

In 1977 Tomes toured with Scotland to the Far East, playing in the 74–9 victory over Japan. He played against New Zealand in both Tests of the 1981 tour but one of the great moments of his career came a year later in Australia when he captained the Scottish XV against Queensland Country (44–16).

Tomes, who once came out firmly in favour of a knock-out cup competition for the top Scottish clubs, names fishing among his main diversions.

ALISTER CAMPBELL
Lock

FULL NAME Alister James Campbell
BORN 1 January 1959 at Hawick
CLUB Hawick

OCCUPATION Bricklayer
HEIGHT 6 ft 4 in
WEIGHT 16 st 2 lb
EDUCATION Burnfoot Primary School; Hawick High School
FIRST CAPPED v Ireland, 1984 at Lansdowne Road
STATUS Married, to Susan
SCOTLAND RECORD won 2, drawn 0, lost 1. Points: none

Alister Campbell is unique among the Grand Slam heroes in that he had never toured abroad with Scotland prior to that historic season. His first taste of that came, in fact, on the Rumanian expedition in May 1984.

The forty-fifth player from the Hawick club to be capped, Campbell's call to arms came when Bill Cuthbertson pulled out injured a week before the Irish game. His rawness never showed

Alister Campbell in the course of a great first game for Scotland. *Bob Thomas*

in the cauldron of excitement at Lansdowne Road and he kept his place for the two subsequent internationals against France and behind the Iron Curtain.

Campbell, or 'Sally', a nickname stemming from his Burnfoot Primary School days, graduated to the Hawick ranks through the PSA semi-junior club and then Hawick Linden. His first game in the coveted green jersey came as a 17-year-old against Howe of Fife and he credits two former Hawick caps, Derrick Grant and Norman Suddon, as being particularly helpful in his career.

A member of the South Inter-District Grand Slam teams of 1983 and 1984, his debut at that level came in 1980 against Leinster on the short Irish tour. The same year he also appeared in a Scottish trial as a 19-year-old.

Campbell faced the Rumanians in South colours at Melrose in 1981 and the following season turned out against Fiji. In 1983 he came on as a replacement for Iain Paxton against the All Blacks at Netherdale. Three B caps came his way, the first against France at Dundee in 1983 and late the same year he shared in the victory over Ireland at Melrose.

Widely experienced as a No. 8 as well as a lock, Alister has a younger brother, Kevin, who has represented South Under-21s in addition to playing for Hawick.

JOHN BEATTIE
No. 8, Flank forward or Lock

FULL NAME John Ross Beattie
BORN 27 November 1957 in North Borneo
CLUB Glasgow Academicals
OCCUPATION Civil Engineer
HEIGHT 6 ft 3¾ in
WEIGHT 15st 4 lb
EDUCATION Uplands School, Malaya; Drumley House Preparatory School; Glasgow Academy; Glasgow University
FIRST CAPPED v Ireland, 1980 at Lansdowne Road
MAJOR TOURS British Lions to South Africa, 1980; British Lions to New Zealand, 1983; Scotland to Rumania, 1984
STATUS Married, to Jill
SCOTLAND RECORD won 5, drawn 1, lost 7. Points: none

John Beattie on the drive against the All Blacks with (left to right) Iain Paxton, Colin Deans and Roy Laidlaw in alert attendance. *Dave Stranock*

John Beattie is the only player who appeared in the Scotland Grand Slam team fortified by the experiences of two British Lions tours: he went to South Africa in 1980 and New Zealand three years later.

His contribution to the 1984 championship was restricted to one half of the Calcutta Cup victory over England, coming off the bench to pack down at second row when Bill Cuthbertson retired hurt. Besides enabling him to help Scotland to a vital 18–9 victory, it was another chance for Beattie to underline his utility value, since he had also gained a cap as a flanker against New Zealand in 1983, in addition to eleven caps in his preferred role of No. 8.

He played in that position throughout the 1980 and 1981 championships and outstanding performances in his first four games earned a ticket to South Africa with the Lions. Although he started out in the Saturday XV, his lack of experience and, reputedly, of confidence overtook him and ultimately he missed out on the Tests, appearing in eight matches and punctuating his displays against Country Districts at Windhoek and Griqualand West at Kimberley with tries.

On the 1983 Lions tour, where he scored four tries – against Wanganui, West Coast and two against Wairarapa Bush – Beattie finally tasted Test action, but as a replacement for Iain Paxton when the second international at Wellington was lost by a 9–0 margin. Beattie had, of course, been unable to tour New Zealand with Scotland in 1981 when he broke a kneecap in training.

He started the 1980–81 season with Heriot's FP during a period of working as a civil engineer – he has a BSc degree – in Edinburgh. That season apart, his senior career has been with Glasgow Academicals where his two younger brothers, Duncan and Allan, also play. But he must have taken some ribbing in the West about playing in an Edinburgh XV which lost 18–19 to Glasgow at Myreside, one of four appearances Beattie made in the capital's colours.

John Beattie's first game for Glasgow Academicals First XV was as an 18-year-old against Stewart's Melville in the national leagues and his Glasgow district debut came when he was hurriedly drafted in at lock for a match against Lancashire three seasons later. He kept his place, appearing against the 1979 All Blacks at Hughenden.

Born in North Borneo where his father was working as a planter, he had his first schooling at Penang in Malaya. He returned to Scotland as a 10-year-old and played for West of Scotland preparatory schools while at Drumley House. His father, John Beattie senior, was a flanker with Queen's Park (now merged with Cartha) and his uncle, Peter Beattie, turned out for the West of Scotland.

Originally, Beattie played stand-off or full-back but, on going to Glasgow Academy, he represented the Glasgow Schools in the pack, benefiting from coaching received from Lachie Robertson. In more recent years, Colin Guthrie has also played a part in shaping his career.

A member of the cricket First XI at school, Beattie demonstrated on the 1984 Rumanian tour what a wizard he is on the electric guitar, having formerly played in rock bands in the Glasgow area.

JIM CALDER
Flank forward

FULL NAME James Hamilton Calder
BORN 20 August 1957 at Haddington

CLUB Stewart's Melville
OCCUPATION Sales Executive
HEIGHT 6 ft
WEIGHT 14 st 10 lb
EDUCATION Knox Academy; Melville College; Heriot Watt
University
FIRST CAPPED v France, 1981 at Parc de Princes
MAJOR TOURS Scotland to France, 1980; Scotland to New
Zealand, 1981; Scotland to Australia, 1982; British Lions to
New Zealand, 1983
STATUS Married, to Lynn
SCOTLAND RECORD won 12, drawn 2, lost 9. Points: 12, from
three tries

Jim Calder is one of four rugby-playing brothers, all with the
Stewart's Melville club, including his twin, Finlay, who is the
younger by thirty minutes. More notable still, Jim, Gavin, Finlay
and John all represented the Scottish Schools, John captaining the
side against Wales and Australia in 1973–74. It was the following
season that Jim and Finlay were capped while Gavin was honoured
in 1970.

A prop in his early rugby days, Calder soon switched to his
present position, wing forward. It was appropriate that his first
cap should have come against France in 1981 for he was in a
Scottish Schools side which crossed the channel and, in 1979, he
had played in all three of Edinburgh's games on a short tour to
Narbonne (16–38), Perpignan (16–10) and Roussillon (15–13).

In 1980, he was selected to undertake a three-match tour with
Scotland to France sandwiched between trips to the Hong Kong
sevens with the Co-optimists and to Canada with his club.

Jim appeared in two winning internationals, against Ireland in
1979 and France in 1980, before being promoted to the full
Scotland side. Once having broken through, he went on to play in
23 successive games, the run being broken only when a back injury
ruled him out of the post Grand Slam tour of Rumania.

Employed in the medical supplies industry and son of Robin
Calder, the former Haddington full-back, Calder's season in a
Scotland jersey was crowned with a tour of New Zealand where
he played in six matches, including both Tests. In 1982 he was
joined by his twin brother, Finlay, on the tour of Australia and
later John was flown out as a replacement, thus bringing forth
comparisons with the Australian trio of Ella brothers, Glen, Garry
and Mark.

Jim Calder on the burst versus Wales. *George Herringshaw*

On the British Lions tour of New Zealand he played in seven of the first fourteen games, scoring tries against Southland, North Auckland and Mid Canterbury, before he broke a thumb during the Third Test, which rendered him a virtual spectator for the remainder of the trip.

Since breaking through into the Scottish side, Calder has scored three tries: against England in 1981, Wales in 1982 and one from a line-out in the dying moments of the match with France which decided the Grand Slam.

Calder played fully a season in the Stewart's/Melville Second XV before making his debut against Musselburgh in a match played under the Stoneyhill floodlights. He is currently captain of the club, for the first time, a post he held with his school XV. Since making his inter-district debut in 1978 in a convincing win over Glasgow at Inverleith, Calder has played 31 times for Edinburgh prior to 1984–85.

A BA graduate in Economics, he played cricket for his school First XI and is an occasional golfer. He married Lynn McAlpine, a PE teacher, on Friday, 13 July 1984.

DAVID LESLIE
Flank forward

FULL NAME David George Leslie
BORN 14 April 1952 at Dundee
CLUB Gala
OCCUPATION Architect
HEIGHT 6ft 1 in
WEIGHT 14 st 7 lb
EDUCATION Dundee High Primary School; Dalhousie
Preparatory School, Glenalmond; Dundee University
FIRST CAPPED v Ireland, 1975 at Murrayfield
MAJOR TOURS Scotland to New Zealand, 1975 and 1981;
Scotland to Rumania, 1984
STATUS Married, to Pamela with son Rodric and daughter
Rebeca
SCOTLAND RECORD won 13, drawn 1, lost 14. Points: 8, from
two tries

But for injuries, David Leslie, who captained the Scottish Schools
against England and Wales in 1970, would undoubtedly have had
more than the 28 caps with which he finished the Grand Slam
season in Rumania, where he notched his second international try
to add to the one scored against England in 1976.

Leslie, in fact, gained six caps in his first year of international
rugby, commencing in February 1975, and, by the time his thir-
teenth appearance came along, against Wales in 1981, he had
played five times for Scotland as a No. 8, his debut berth, and
seven times on the flank. In recent years all Leslie's international
appearances have been as a wing forward.

First capped out of Dundee High School, when they were in
Division Four, Leslie also represented Scotland during his days
with West of Scotland. After joining Gala in 1978, he captained
them to their third official Scottish championship. Consequently,
he has played for three districts, North Midlands, for whom he
made his debut in 1973, Glasgow and the South.

His first game for Gala was against Boroughmuir in October
1978. By the start of the 1984–85 season, he had represented them
98 times, scoring 41 tries, including four against Gordonians in
1980, at that time a record for a Gala forward in a first-class
match.

David Leslie at full stretch versus France. *All Sport*

Captain of the Whites team which defeated the Blues in the national trial, Leslie played in 1984 as if he had a point to prove to the Lions selectors, who had omitted him from the 1983 New Zealand tour. Recognition of his outstanding performances came during the close season when readers of *Rugby World* magazine voted him the Top Player of the Championship, one place ahead of his club-mate Jim Aitken.

Besides visiting South Africa in 1983 with a Five Nations Championship side to mark the centenary of the Western Province Rugby Union, Leslie has twice toured New Zealand with Scotland. He played in five of the seven matches in 1975 and, on the 1981 tour, was handed the captaincy for matches against Wellington (15–19) and Mid Canterbury (23–12).

Selected to tour Australia with Scotland in 1982, he had to withdraw from the party since it came too soon after the broken leg he had sustained in a national league fixture with Heriot's FP at Goldenacre. He was twice a B international, against France in 1974 at Bayonne and at Melrose in 1975, and it is interesting that this world-class breakaway was still playing stand-off at the age of fifteen.

His father was general manager of a Dundee-based newspaper concern. His older brother, Roger, a former North and Midlands player, has undoubtedly been one of the major influences upon his rugby career.

An honours graduate in architecture, David Leslie is now based once again in Dundee, having spent some time living and working in Galashiels.

IAIN PAXTON
No. 8

FULL NAME Iain Angus McLeod Paxton
BORN 29 December 1957 in Dunfermline
CLUB Selkirk
OCCUPATION Building Society Representative
HEIGHT 6 ft 4 in
WEIGHT 15 st 7 lb
EDUCATION Sinclairtown and Burntisland Primary Schools; Kirkcaldy High School; Beath High School
FIRST CAPPED v New Zealand, 1981 at Dunedin
MAJOR TOURS Scotland to New Zealand, 1981; Scotland to Australia, 1982; British Lions to New Zealand, 1983
STATUS Single
SCOTLAND RECORD won 10, drawn 2, lost 5. Points: 4, from one try

Opportunity knocked for Iain Paxton at the end of the 1981 season when he was called into the Scotland squad for the tour of New Zealand after John Beattie had broken a kneecap in training. Although Derek White of Gala had been preferred a short time earlier, when the other No. 8 originally selected for the party, Peter Lillington – then at Durham University – pulled out because of exams, Paxton really made the most of his opportunity. He made his Test debut in the 11–4 defeat at Dunedin and played also in the Test at Auckland a week later (15–40).

There followed a further ten successive caps at No. 8, including the two Tests in Australia in 1982, a tour which saw him make just four appearances. He was dropped for the visit to France in 1983 and then re-instated, albeit at lock, for the Calcutta Cup victory at Twickenham two matches later.

Although he also turned out in the second row for the match against the Barbarians, Paxton played throughout the 1984 international season as No. 8 until the tour of Rumania, which he missed owing to his examinations in computer science. A short time later, he gave up his studies to work as a representative with the Bristol and West Building Society, where he is under Gordon Brown, the former Scotland and Lions lock.

A former Under-18 schools basketball cap, who previously played with the Dunfermline Pagans, Paxton has a Hebridean mother, from Lewis, while his father, from East Lothian, rose to the rank of Chief Superintendent in the police.

Iain Paxton those few inches higher than Jean-Luc Joinel as Jean-Pierre Rives comes round in foiled support. *Bob Thomas*

His early senior rugby was played with Glenrothes where he was helped by Hamish Brown, Bob Wheelan, Norrie Leitch, and Bob Findlay. After making his debut against Waid Academy FP in 1975–76, while still at school, he was part of the club's rise from Division Seven to Division Four in consecutive seasons.

Although his name was closely linked with Heriot's FP for a spell, Paxton eventually decided to take the step up with Selkirk and must have wondered at times what it was like to lose a national league match. In his first season at Philiphaugh, Selkirk swept through the Second Division card undefeated while only Old Aloysians had managed to beat Glenrothes during their otherwise all-conquering surge.

Harry Moultrie and Bob Hutchison are noted as the early schoolboy coaches of the seventh Selkirk player to be capped. Immediately prior to joining Selkirk, Paxton toured Argentina with the Penguins and played in a couple of games before the visit was aborted after two players were arrested for allegedly stealing an Argentinian flag.

In addition to his eleven games for North and Midlands, starting against Penycraig on a tour of Wales, Paxton has also represented the South fifteen times, beginning against Queensland in 1980. His B international career covers just one match, against France in 1979, and his only international try was scored against Wales at Cardiff in 1984 – the first of the Grand Slam campaign.

Paxton played in all four Tests on the 1983 British Lions tour and in five other provincial fixtures, scoring tries against Bay of Plenty (34–16), Manawatu (25–18), Canterbury (20–22) and Hawkes Bay (25–19).

ANDY IRVINE

Full-back (replacement)

FULL NAME Andrew Robertson Irvine
BORN 16 September 1951 in Edinburgh
CLUB Heriot's FP
OCCUPATION Chartered Surveyor
HEIGHT 5 ft 10 in
WEIGHT 12 st 8 lb
EDUCATION James Gillespie's Primary School; George Heriot's Secondary School; Edinburgh University

THE NEW IMMORTALS

Andy Irvine. *George Herringshaw*

FIRST CAPPED v New Zealand, 1972 at Murrayfield
MAJOR TOURS Scotland to New Zealand, 1975; British Lions to
New Zealand, 1977; British Lions to South Africa, 1980;
Scotland to New Zealand, 1981; Scotland to Australia, 1982
STATUS Married, to Audrey with daughters Sarah and Jennifer
SCOTLAND RECORD won 19, drawn 3, lost 29. Points: 273, from
10 tries, 25 conversions and 61 penalties

Andy Irvine, the world record points holder in international rugby,
with 273, has not played for Scotland since setting a new record
of 51 caps (subsequently left behind by Jim Renwick) against
Australia in Sydney in 1982.

Injuries have hampered in recent years the career of this truly
international player. Irvine returned to the international squad for
the Triple Crown encounter with Ireland and the Grand Slam
decider against France at Murrayfield only as a replacement.

Nevertheless, he has much to look back on with pride, starting
with four Scottish Schools caps as a centre while at George Heriot's
School. As a BSc graduate from Edinburgh University, Irvine made
his district debut on the wing against the South at Kelso in January

1971 and has now made exactly 50 appearances in the capital's colours with a total haul of 323 points.

It was as a wing, too, that he made his Lions Test debut, in South Africa, playing twice in the 1974 series, while in all games on that tour he amassed 156 points, a record for a Lion in that country.

He played at full-back in all four Tests for the Lions in New Zealand in 1977 and, in a provincial game against Wanganui-King Country, scored five tries. Originally selected for the 1980 Lions tour of South Africa, he had to drop out at the last moment when he was found to be injured, but recovered to join the party as a replacement and play in the final three Tests. His total number of Lions Test appearances stands at nine and no Scot can claim more.

Without doubt his ability to play either wing or full-back helped him in that respect and, of his 51 Scotland caps, Irvine has four as a winger.

Captain of Heriot's when they won the First Division title in 1979, Irvine led Scotland on fifteen occasions. His enormous contribution to rugby football was recognized with the award of an MBE in June 1979.

DOUG WYLLIE
Stand-off (replacement)

FULL NAME Douglas Stewart Wyllie
BORN 20 May 1963 in Edinburgh
CLUB Stewart's Melville
OCCUPATION Banker
HEIGHT 6 ft 1 in
WEIGHT 13 st
EDUCATION Daniel Stewart's Primary School; Stewart's Melville College
MAJOR TOURS Scotland to Rumania, 1984
STATUS Single

Douglas Wyllie came on to the Scotland bench for the 25–25 draw against New Zealand and continued to understudy John Rutherford throughout the Grand Slam campaign, going also to Rumania where his twenty-first birthday coincided with the Test in Bucharest.

Capped at B level in the wins over Ireland and France in 1983–84, Wyllie made his Edinburgh debut against North and Midlands in Aberdeen in 1982 and has been a district regular ever since, including the match against New Zealand in 1983.

His father is a former player with Dalkeith. The family went to live in London and Hull for spells, during which Wyllie played for an England Schools Under-15 soccer team in an international tournament in the Netherlands, scoring a goal in the victory over West Germany in the final.

STUART JOHNSTON
Scrum-half (replacement)

FULL NAME Stuart Johnston
BORN 20 August 1960 in Edinburgh
CLUB Watsonians
OCCUPATION Trainee Chartered Accountant
HEIGHT 5 ft 10 in
WEIGHT 12 st
EDUCATION George Watson's College
STATUS Single

A scrum-half and younger brother of David Johnston, the international centre, Stuart Johnston arrived on the senior representative scene in 1983–84.

By-passed for Edinburgh's short tour of Middlesex and Kent at the start of the season, Johnston was in the team by Christmas Eve, making a try-scoring debut in the 68–9 thrashing of North Midlands at Murrayfield.

A former Scottish Schools cap, he was under serious consideration for elevation to the full Scotland side when Roy Laidlaw sustained his head injury in Dublin, with the man who replaced Laidlaw at half-time that day, Gordon Hunter, having to be ruled out because of a cheekbone fracture. In the event Laidlaw recovered but Johnston provided cover on the bench for the match against France – the first time he had fulfilled that duty.

Johnston must have come close to touring Rumania, too, for although Hunter recovered, Laidlaw was doubtful right up to the time of departure because of a groin strain.

ROB CUNNINGHAM
Hooker (replacement)

FULL NAME Robert Cunningham
BORN 5 January 1951 in Edinburgh
CLUB Bath
OCCUPATION Building Society representative
HEIGHT 5 ft 10 in
WEIGHT 13 st
EDUCATION Forrester High School, Edinburgh
MAJOR TOURS Scotland to Australia, 1982; Scotland to Rumania, 1984
STATUS Married, to Anne with a son Richard and a daughter Nicola

Rob Cunningham was reserve for all the Grand Slam games except the French visit to Murrayfield when he was suffering from a muscle injury. The Edinburgh-born Cunningham has been on the bench thirteen times in major internationals without managing to achieve that coveted cap and played in matches against Queensland Country, Victoria, New South Wales Country and Capital Territory on the 1982 Australian tour.

A member of the Bath team which in 1983 won the John Player Cup, beating Bristol at Twickenham, he had made a previous appearance in the final with Gosforth. He also played for a spell with Boroughmuir, travelling each week from Tyneside.

Cunningham has the rare distinction of being an RFU senior coach as well as an SRU advisory coach, taking part in summer courses at both Riccarton and Bisham Abbey. His greatest claim to fame is that he led Scotland B in the victories over Ireland and France in 1983–84.

GARY CALLANDER
Hooker (replacement)

FULL NAME Gary Callander
BORN 5 July 1959
CLUB Kelso
OCCUPATION Electrical contractor
HEIGHT 6 ft 1 in
WEIGHT 15 st
EDUCATION Edenside Primary School; Kelso High School
FIRST CAPPED v Rumania, 1984 in Bucharest
MAJOR TOURS Scotland to Rumania, 1984
STATUS Married, to Diana
SCOTLAND RECORD won 0, drawn 0, lost 1

Gary Callander took over as Scotland's reserve hooker from the injured Rob Cunningham for the Grand Slam game with France,

Gary Callander. *Dave Stranock*

the fifth time he had sat on the Scotland bench, including the non-cap match against Fiji in 1982.

Callander had just over two months to wait before becoming the eleventh Kelso international. He gained his first cap on the Rumanian tour when, with Colin Deans unavailable to travel, he edged out Cunningham for the Test slot in Bucharest.

Captain of Kelso in 1982–83, he received a B cap against France in Bourgoin-Jallieu a year earlier, and is a regular member of the talented Kelso seven-a-side team, having gained 22 winners medals from Borders tournaments in addition to three successes in the Haig event at Murrayfield. Callander's sevens prowess also took him to the Cathay Pacific/Hong Kong Bank tournament in 1983.

He hooked for the South against Rumania in 1981–82 and played against Glasgow later that season. With Deans an ever-present in 1982–83, he missed out then on South representative honours but played against Northumberland, Ulster and Durham in the first three matches of last season.

NORRIE ROWAN
Prop (replacement)

FULL NAME Norman Arthur Rowan
BORN 17 September 1951 in Edinburgh
CLUB Boroughmuir
OCCUPATION Builder
HEIGHT 5 ft 10 in
WEIGHT 15 st 7 lb
EDUCATION Forrester School
FIRST CAPPED v Wales, 1980 at Cardiff
MAJOR TOURS Scotland to New Zealand, 1981; Scotland to Australia, 1982; Scotland to Rumania, 1984
STATUS Married, to Pam with son Norman and daughters Lisa and Caroline
SCOTLAND RECORD won 2, drawn 0, lost 5. Points: none

Reserve for all four Grand Slam games, Norrie Rowan hoisted his cap count to seven on the tour of Rumania. His first cap followed appearances for a Scottish XV against Holland at Hilversum in 1977 and Scotland B against France at Le Havre that same year.

At present captain of his club, Boroughmuir, Rowan played in

Norrie Rowan. *Dave Stranock*

three matches on the 1981 New Zealand tour and a similar number
in Australia a year later. He played twice in Rumania.

He played for Scotland against the Barbarians in 1983 in the
match which officially opened the new Murrayfield East stand and
he has toured abroad with both the Saltires and the Penguins.

He was played as a flanker when he joined Boroughmuir from
Forrester FP eleven years ago, having occasionally turned out on
the wing. Boroughmuir's fifth international behind Ken Ross,
Bill Watson, Bruce Hay and Graham Hogg, he is an established
tight-head prop who did, however, play on the loose-head against
Rumania for Edinburgh in 1979.